DR. TONY KEMERLY
and STEVE SNYDER

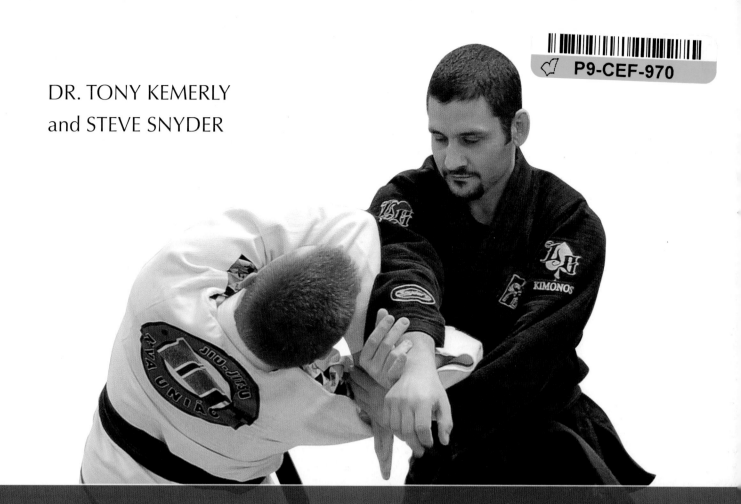

TAEKWONDO
GRAPPLING TECHNIQUES

Hone Your Competitive Edge For **Mixed Martial Arts**

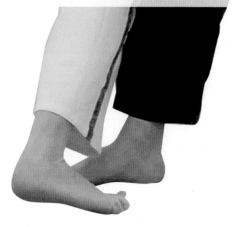

TUTTLE PUBLISHING
Tokyo • Rutland, Vermont • Singapore

Published by Tuttle Publishing, an imprint of Periplus Editions (HK) Ltd., with editorial offices at 364 Innovation Drive, North Clarendon, Vermont 05759 U.S.A.

Library of Congress Cataloging-in-Publication Data

Kemerly, Tony.
  Taekwondo grappling techniques : hone your competitive edge for mixed martial arts / Tony Kemerly, Steve Snyder.
    p. cm.
  ISBN 978-0-8048-4006-4 (pbk.)
  1. Tae kwon do. 2. Hand-to-hand fighting, Oriental. 3. Mixed martial arts. I. Snyder, Steve. II. Title.
  GV1114.9.K46 2009
  796.815'3--dc22
               2008053309

DISTRIBUTED BY

North America, Latin America & Europe
Tuttle Publishing
364 Innovation Drive
North Clarendon, VT 05759-9436 U.S.A.
Tel: 1 (802) 773-8930; Fax: 1 (802) 773-6993
info@tuttlepublishing.com
www.tuttlepublishing.com

Japan
Tuttle Publishing
Yaekari Building, 3rd Floor
5-4-12 Osaki, Shinagawa-ku
Tokyo 141 0032
Tel: (81) 3 5437-0171; Fax: (81) 3 5437-0755
tuttle-sales@gol.com

Asia Pacific
Berkeley Books Pte. Ltd.
61 Tai Seng Avenue #02-12
Singapore 534167
Tel: (65) 6280-1330; Fax: (65) 6280-6290
inquiries@periplus.com.sg
www.periplus.com

First edition
13 12 11 10 09   5 4 3 2 1

Printed in Singapore

TUTTLE PUBLISHING® is a registered trademark of Tuttle Publishing, a division of Periplus Editions (HK) Ltd.

ACKNOWLEDGMENTS

I would like to thank my wife Trish for all of her photography skills (free of charge), time, and heartfelt enthusiasm for this project. Without her, this project would not have gotten off of the ground. — Dr. Tony Kemerly

I would like to thank my close friends Trish and Tony "Doc" Kemerly for all their continued support over the years; LDMA dedicated students who make teaching martial arts exciting every day; Mr. Danny Dring for always being a good friend, coach, and motivating me to reach higher levels in martial arts; Most of all, to my wife, Mariea, and children, Deven and Elizabeth, for supporting me and making everything in life complete. — Steve Snyder

DEDICATION

We dedicate this book to all of our students and fellow martial artists in their continued pursuit of excellence in the martial arts.

I would like to dedicate this book to Mr. Danny Dring, Mr. Berl Parsons, Mr. Joe Lewis, Mr. Bill "Superfoot" Wallace, Mr. Allen Branch, Mr. Rick Hoadley, and Mrs. Mariea Snyder; you are my heroes. I have great appreciation for everything you have done to influence and expand my knowledge in martial arts. — Steve Snyder

CONTENTS

CHAPTER

1

Taekwondo's History as a Foundation for its Grappling Techniques

The history of the Korean martial art Taekwondo is questionable to say the least. Multiple histories of Taekwondo exist. The history described simply depends on the individual telling it. One of the more dubious histories of Taekwondo is the Taekkyon Derivation History. The Taekkyon Derivation History holds that Taekwondo is the direct descendant of the Korean folk game Taekkyon. Taekkyon and sport Taekwondo do share some similarities such as a penchant for circular kicking techniques, the palms for pushing the opponent, and well-developed leg jams, sweeps, and leg traps. Taekkyon all but disappeared at the start of the 20th century because it was linked with crime and vengeance and was therefore shunned by the Korean people. This version of Taekwondo's history still persists due to the fact that Taekkyon is a uniquely Korean martial art with no outside influences. This is an important factor for the extremely nationalistic Korean people. However, Taekkyon didn't resurface publicly until the 1970s, many years after Taekwondo was in existence. Despite the desire for a uniquely Korean history, the veracity of this version of Taekwondo's history remains questionable at best.

Taekwondo History and Development— The Shotokan Connection

Regardless of the romantic nature of the Taekkyon Derivation Theory, most Taekwondo practitioners accept the fact that their art is a Korean version of Shotokan Karate-do or Kongsoodo in Korean. Even the name Taekwondo is only a little more than 50 years old, having been developed by a group of masters on April 11, 1955. The Japanese martial arts have had an influence on Korean martial arts for some time. In fact, until the year 1909, all Korean boys learned the Japanese arts Judo and Kendo while in school. Before the Korean War, the original kwans or schools used the name karate along with Japanese terminology and Japanese kata from the Shotokan, Shorin-ryu and Shorei-ryu schools.

The individual kwans that were eventually united to form Taekwondo were led by men who received most if not all of their martial training from the Japanese martial arts. The Chung Do Kwan or Great Blue Wave School, which became the largest of the civilian kwans, was founded in 1945 by Won Kuk Lee. Lee earned his black belt from the founder of Shotokan Karate, Gichin Funakoshi. He also trained in Okinawa, Henan, and Shanghai. The Chung Do Kwan taught that movements should mimic the power of water. The Moo Duk Kwan or School of Martial Virtue was founded in 1945 by Hwang Kee. Kee received martial arts training in Manchuria under Tai Chi master Kuk Jin Yang. The Yun Moo Kwan or Way of Wisdom School, which later became the Ji Do Kwan was founded in 1946 by Chan Sup Sang. Sang began his martial arts education in Judo and began by teaching Taekwondo to Judo black belts. This school was the first mixed martial arts school as karate and judo were taught there. The school patch of the Yun Moo Kwan is very similar to the Shotokan patch as a tribute to its source. The Chang Do Kwan was founded in 1946 by Byung Yun, a 4th degree black belt in the Okinawan Shudokan karate style under Kanken Toyama and Nam Suk Lee, who learned Okinawan Shotokan Karate from an old Chinese text on the subject. This school was considered to be the premier self-defense method in post-war Korea, quite different from today's modern Taekwondo. The Song Moo Kwan or Ever Youthful House of Martial Arts Training, was founded in 1946 by Byong-Jik Ro, a contemporary of Won Kuk Lee, the founder of the Chung Do Kwan. Ro earned his black belt in Shotokan Karate under its founder Gichin Funakoshi. To further illustrate its roots, The "Song" in Song Moo Kwan refers to Song Do Kwan, the Korean name for Shotokan. Lastly, the Oh Do Kwan or School of My Way, was founded in 1953 by Choi Hong Hi who held a 2nd degree black belt in Shotokan Karate and Nam Tae Hi. The Oh Do Kwan was militaristic in nature and was a product of the Republic of Korea's army. This kwan was closely linked to the Chung Do Kwan, of which Nam Tae Hi was a member. These early kwans that eventually became Taekwondo were obviously influenced by the Japanese martial arts. This is because the men who played a large part in the development of Taekwondo had their foundation in Japanese martial arts.

Taekwondo—Sport versus Traditional

The change of the martial roots of Taekwondo occurred when the leaders of the Korean Taekwondo movement began to try to make the art of Karate their own. It was also at this time that the style itself splintered into two main factions: Sport Taekwondo, which is today under the auspices of the World Taekwondo Federation (WTF) and Traditional Taekwondo, which is under the control of the International Taekwondo Federation (ITF). This split occurred for a simple reason. After the end of the Korean occupation by the Japanese, Korean martial arts changed into a combination of Chinese, Japanese, and Okinawan hand techniques mixed with Chinese, Japanese, Okinawan, and Taekkyon kicking techniques. This continued after the Korean War when a wave of nationalism and patriotism within Korea led to a "Koreanization" of Japanese karate. This "Koreanization" consisted of changing Japanese names to Korean alternatives. This is often seen in the naming of patterns such as: (Japanese → Korean) Heian → Pyong-An; Tekki → Chul-gi; Bassai → Pal-sek; Kanku Dai → Kong Sang Koon; Jitte → Ship-Soo; Empi → Yoon-bi; and many other examples. It is through the denial of the Japanese roots of Shotokan inherent within Taekwondo that the Taekkyon Derivation theory gained momentum, however flawed it may be.

The final step of the "Koreanization" of Shotokan was the creation of a set of techniques that were significantly different from those found in Shotokan. This was accomplished by the competition rule set found in today's "Olympic-style" Taekwondo sparring. This system was actually opposed by the 1st generation masters who held to their link to Shotokan. The reason that the masters didn't like the change was simply that the changes removed the self-defense aspect of their art, in essence making it a game of tag, much like the uniquely Korean Taekkyon. The rules of the new Korean Taekwondo were as follows: no strikes to the face; no strikes below the waist; no grabbing; mandatory body protection; a scoring system; and continuous fighting. The result of these changes was the elimination of all grappling and controlling techniques, effectively relegating the self-defense aspect of the art to the ability of the practitioner to keep an attacker at bay, primarily through kicking techniques.

The "Koreanization" of the art resulted in a few other changes to the philosophy of the art. For example, traditional Taekwondo uses an attack → block → counterattack methodology for self-defense. This was eliminated when Taekwondo adopted a sporting outlook as the new Taekwondo adopted an attack → counterattack. The adoption of the new attack → counterattack method eliminates the need for blocking, which eliminates a key period of defensive contact that allows for a transition into grappling techniques. Another difference between sport and traditional Taekwondo that lends itself to the premise of inherent grappling techniques in Taekwondo is a difference in mindset that's exhibited between the two versions of the art.

The purpose of sport Taekwondo is to perform a technique correctly so that you are able to score more points than your opponent and thereby win the match. This philosophy greatly differs from that of traditional Taekwondo that adopts a mindset much more like its Japanese predecessors. The purpose of traditional Taekwondo is to perform a technique correctly so that you may disable or kill an opponent. The implementation of this purpose requires that grappling techniques be present in a style. It is true that striking techniques are able to disable or kill an attacker, but not nearly so quickly or efficiently as grappling techniques. Lastly, don't forget that one of the early Kwans, the Oh Do Kwan, was a military body that needed efficient disabling and killing techniques on the battlefield. And the leader of the Oh Do Kwan, General Choi Hong Hi, was the head of the International Taekwondo Federation, essentially the governing body of Traditional Taekwondo.

Understanding Taekwondo Patterns

One of the unique characteristics of the martial arts is the practice of patterns. These patterns, hyung, tul, or poomse in Korean, kata in Japanese, quyen in Vietnamese, or taolu in Chinese, are a prearranged series of different defensive, counter, and offensive techniques performed in a precise, logical sequence with specific foot movements and stances in imaginary combat against a number of assailants. To the uninitiated, these patterns resemble a combination of shadowboxing, dancing, and gymnastics floor exercises. These patterns are thought to represent the martial traditions and techniques of a specific martial art. Performance of patterns results in stronger, faster, and more effective kicks, blocks, strikes, and stances; improved fighting techniques; defensive and offensive techniques for self-defense situations; increased endurance, both muscular and cardiovascular; increased rhythm and agility; and better kinesthetic awareness.

The art of Taekwondo is often characterized as a martial art that uses powerful, yet unrealistic kicking techniques for combat. While it is true that Taekwondo does possess an arsenal of flashy kicking techniques, that characterization is quite superficial. If you were to examine the patterns used by practitioners of Taekwondo, you would find certain movements that could be interpreted as grappling techniques. Lower belt patterns tend to have more fist movements and long range techniques that may be viewed as grabbing and entering techniques, whereas high belt patterns have more open hand and close range movements that represent grappling and infighting. All of the patterns utilize an action-reaction principle in their movements. This action-reaction movement greatly resembles off-balancing techniques utilized in arts like judo or jujutsu.

A Brief History of Patterns

In order to see that Taekwondo has grappling techniques embedded in its patterns, we must first examine the patterns of Shotokan Karate, the style that most agree has had the greatest influence on Taekwondo's techniques and development.

During the 11th century, many Japanese warriors fled to Okinawa as a result of the devastation of the Taira-Minamoto wars. The warriors of the Minamoto clan believed that all movement was the same. Therefore practitioners of their art, Minamoto Bujitsu, believed that any type of combat, be it striking, grappling, or using weapons all relied on similar movements. Students of this style would be taught a combative movement. Once they had mastered that movement, they were shown how it relates to striking, grappling, or weapons usage. We see this same pretense today in Japanese Aikido and jujutsu, Filipino Kali, and Vietnamese Thanh Long where sword, stick, or knife techniques double as joint-locking and takedown techniques when the weapon is removed from the practitioner's hands.

In 1377, the king of Okinawa pledged allegiance to China. The result of this union was a flood of Chinese custom and culture into the country of Okinawa. Specifically, there was the immigration of 36 Chinese families. This group of families included many experts in the Chinese art Kempo or "Fist Law." The art of Kempo combined with the native Okinawan art Te to form today's Okinawan Karate or Okinawa-te. Later, in 1429, King Sho Hashi began to trade with other countries, including Indonesia, Southeast Asia, Korea, Japan, and China which resulted in the cities of Naha and Shuri becoming major trading centers. The opening of trade with these other countries resulted in the martial arts of these other countries becoming available to the people of Okinawa. These countries, had their own indigenous martial arts, but Indonesia, Southeast Asia, and China specifically had martial arts with extensive grappling in their repertoire. About 50 years later in 1477, King Sho Shin banned all private weapon ownership which acted as a driving force for the Okinawan people to greatly develop their empty-hand fighting skills. Finally, about 130 years later in 1609, the Satsuma clan invaded Okinawa at the behest of the Tokugawa shogunate. This invasion resulted in the an even greater advancement of the empty-hand fighting skills of the Okinawan people as their art became extremely violent, as its purpose was to quickly disable and kill an armed and possible armored attacker through the use of powerful striking techniques as well as bone breaking and joint disruption techniques. It is at this point in the history of the Japanese/Okinawan martial arts, most of the patterns that were taught were of Chinese origin. These patterns contained highly effective and brutal fighting techniques loaded with Chin-na or Chinese joint-locking techniques.

In 1868 however, this all changed. Japan moved from a feudalistic government to a democratic one that resulted in a few changes to the martial arts. The martial arts began to be taught as a way to promote the values of the past. This was done by using the martial arts to foster health, spirit, morality, and national identity, instead of the most efficient way to disable an opponent. Finally, a sportification of Japanese martial arts began. This switch to a more holistic, sporting martial art gained ground in 1908 when Itosu "Anko" Yasutsune was able to incorporate karate training into the physical education programs in all elementary schools on Okinawa. In order to do this however, a few changes needed to be made to the art. For these changes, he was often criticized for effectively watering down the combat efficacy of karate. He disguised the more dangerous techniques, i.e. grappling, and taught the art as one primarily based on blocking and punching. No combative application was taught for any technique, meaning the patterns were taught without their application thereby making them no different than any of the traditional dances popular at the time. Lastly, deceptive names were given to the techniques that were taught, such as "high block" or "low block". Prior to this, what we know as a "high block" or "low block" was utilized as a striking or grappling technique in addition to its role in blocking. It is now clear that karate patterns did at one time contain more than just striking and blocking techniques.

Taekwondo Patterns

Today's Taekwondo patterns, specifically those used by Traditional Taekwondo practitioners, share many similarities with the older Japanese patterns. The original Okinawan Pinan pattern set and the newer Heian set are thought to be watered-down versions of the Kanku Dai (Kusanku) pattern. The Heian set was changed by Itosu to make them easier to learn by introducing easier techniques first. These patterns are still taught today in some Traditional Taekwondo schools under the Pyong-Ahn name. Early Traditional Taekwondo did not emphasize sparring as the art was still considered to be for self-defense purposes. The techniques in these patterns were not meant to be used to teach sport fighting; instead, these patterns were to be used by a soldier in battle and were meant to be used against aggressive, untrained attackers, which is why the applications of the patterns emphasize close-range self-defense techniques.

When Traditional Taekwondo and Shotokan patterns are compared, many similarities may be found. For example, the following Japanese patterns have a nearly identical Korean counterpart: Kanku Dai and Kong-Soo-Kan; Tekki and Chul-Gi; Bassai and Pal-Sek; Jion and Jaon; and Empi and Unbi. Other patterns are not identical, but similar movement patterns are found in the following: Heian Nidan and Won-Hyo; Tekki Shodan, Nidan, and Sandan and the Chang-Hon pattern Po-Eun; and Heian Shodan and the Chang-Hon patterns Chon-Ji and Dan-Gun.

The Chang-Hon patterns were the first "original" Taekwondo patterns and were developed by General Choi Hong Hi. The movements in these patterns have a large Shotokan influence, which is not a surprise considering General Choi received his 2nd degree black belt in Shotokan Karate while in Japan. Techniques found within the Chang-Hon patterns include throws, takedowns, chokes, strangles, joint locks of the wrist, elbow, finger, leg, and neck, and some ground fighting techniques. This pattern set is unique in that it contains complex footwork patterns in the nine under-black belt patterns. This intricate footwork is the basis for the grappling techniques in the patterns. Many of the Chang-Hon patterns are quite long and contain hand and foot combinations that do not often seem to make sense. These seemingly nonsensical combinations often tend to have grappling applications. It is through a thorough examination of the Chang-Hon patterns that we will find Taekwondo's hidden grappling techniques.

A Brief History of Japanese Jujutsu and Brazilian Jiu-jitsu

The history of Japanese jujutsu is as interesting as that of its striking counterpart. Of course, when something is as old as an art like jujutsu, its history becomes more than a little muddled. For example, depending on the researcher, the roots of Japanese jujutsu come from ancient Greek grappling systems like Pankration, older Mongolian grappling arts, or simply that jujutsu is completely Japanese in its roots and has not been diluted by the native arts of other lands since its inception. The concern of this section is not to argue which history is most accurate and which is most self-serving, rather it is to illustrate a connection between older Japanese jujutsu and the corresponding Brazilian jiu-jitsu.

One of the largest misconceptions about Japanese jujutsu is that it was always practiced as a stand-alone art. This art, which has been known as jujutsu, taijutsu, wajutsu, torite, and yawara existed as an art that balanced the use of empty hand skills with weapons skills so that it would be useful to the samurai. A purely empty hand martial art would not be useful to the samurai because they fought as armed soldiers, much like soldiers of today. It is for this very reason that today's military does not spend a great deal of time teaching hand-to-hand combat because of the many weapons a soldier has at his disposal. Because of the use of weapons by the samurai, jujutsu was at best an ancillary skill utilized in a worst-case scenario.

It was in the late 19th century that a slightly built man by the name of Jigoro Kano developed a system he called Judo. It is important to note that Judo is nothing more than another style of jujutsu and not a separate martial art. In point of fact, Kano was not even the first individual to use the name judo. Kano's Judo was a system that he developed after mastering the Tenjin Shinyo-ryu, Kito-ryu, and Fusen-ryu styles of jujutsu. After his years of jujutsu training, Kano felt that that an underlying philosophy behind the jujutsu arts was lacking. It was because jujutsu was more a collection of techniques than a philosophical art that Kano decided to develop an art of his own that had some underlying principle on which the entire system was based. The principle that he decided upon was one simply to force your opponent to lose his balance, then attack. As simplistic as that may sound, it still is the base for the underlying strategy of Judo, which is to use minimal effort to achieve maximal efficiency.

One of the most important contributions to the martial arts, and especially Judo and indirectly, Brazilian jiu-jitsu, was the concept of randori or free sparring. Randori is simply a method of sparring that allows practitioners to practice their techniques in a safe manner while performing them realistically. In the early days of Judo, the use of randori allowed Kano's students to practice more often since they were not constantly injured or trying to recover from some injury as a result of an overly aggressive training session in jujutsu. Basically, randori watered down Judo so that it could be practiced often, without making the art useless for self-defense or sport endeavors. It is this type of randori that separates modern Brazilian jiu-jitsu from many other martial arts and allows its students to excel.

The road that led Judo to be the foundation for Brazilian jiu-jitsu began late in the 19th century when a match between the older jujutsu styles and Kano's new Judo was arranged at the Tokyo Police Station. Because of their use of randori and their ability to practice their techniques more often, the practitioners of Kano's Judo successfully defeated the practitioners of the older styles of jujutsu. After the victory at the Tokyo Police Station, Judo grew in popularity as a result of more victories in tournaments and challenge matches. This seemingly invincible streak continued until around 1900 when Kano's school, the Kodokan, challenged the Fusen-ryu school to a challenge match. The Fusen-ryu practitioners knew that they would not be able to defeat the Judo players because they did not posses the throwing skills that the judoka possessed. As a result, they took them to the ground and won the matches by submission. This loss was the first that the Kodokan had suffered in approximately eight years. Up until this time, Judo did not have a grappling component, so after the loss, Kano decided that that aspect of his art was sorely needed. As a result, he blended the techniques of the Fusen-ryu with his art of Judo.

The loss to the Fusen-ryu dojo served to shape the style of Brazilian jiu-jitsu as we know it today. The implementation of grappling techniques to the Judo curriculum occurred shortly before Judo reached the shores of Brazil. This is thought to be one of the main reasons why Brazilian jiu-jitsu has such an extensive focus on grappling. In 1904 a Japanese judoka trained by Kano himself, Mitsuo Maeda, traveled to the United States with his instructor to demonstrate the art of Judo to the cadets at West Point as well as to the President of the United States who at that time was Theodore Roosevelt. After Maeda left the United States, he continued his travels to Brazil as it was at the time the largest Japanese settlement outside of Japan. One of the men that aided him in his efforts while he was there was Gastao Gracie. As thanks for his help, Maeda taught Gracie's son, Carlos, the basics of Kano's Judo. In turn, Carlos taught his brothers, among them, Helio Gracie. As a result, Brazilian jiu-jitsu was born.

How to Use This Book

Finding the grappling techniques in Taekwondo patterns may at first glance seem difficult, but with practice this is not so. Here are a few examples that may open your mind to a few new possibilities. Kicking chambers and re-chambers could be sweeps or ground techniques rather than kicking techniques. Do not assume that the attackers we are battling in our patterns only attack us with strikes. Try to imagine the movements performed horizontally or on some other plane rather than from a standing position. Do not assume that the labels assigned to techniques, such as "high block" or "middle block" apply to the techniques. Remember, these names were only added in the past 100 years. Remove the technique from the flow of the pattern and see if other applications could apply. Ask yourself why things are they way they are. For example: why a palm strike rather than a fist attack; why does a stance change from a forward to a back or sitting stance or vice versa; why all the different chambers for hand techniques? So, in order to find the grappling in your patterns, simply utilize some abstract thought and keep an open mind throughout the process.

It is important to understand that many of the early masters we try to emulate were firm believers in cross-training methodologies. Those who excelled in striking arts often knew how to grapple and vice versa. When we fast-forward to the present, we find martial arts fragmented at best. Striking arts believe that they have the keys to the kingdom while grappling arts feel the same way. Furthermore, reality-based self-defense arts feel like traditional martial arts have lost their way during modern times and reality-based self-defense practitioners are the ones with the secrets of old. The purpose of this book is not to say with complete certainty that the grappling techniques in the Chang-Hon patterns are decidedly fact; rather that the movements within those forms can double as grappling techniques. It is by training in both striking and grappling that many of these techniques have presented themselves to me through the course of my training. So try to find some techniques in your own patterns and have fun.

CHAPTER 2

Grappling in Blocking Techniques

Square Block

TECHNIQUE

Square Block – Execution

APPLICATION

The grappling application of the square block becomes evident when it is performed from a horizontal position. White has taken the side control position on Black. From this position, White will be able to control Black's movement while setting up many different submission techniques. Black places the high block portion of the square block under White's chin and the forearm block portion under his hips. By doing this, Black does not let White lock down the position on him and he is able to move his hips away and escape.

Square Block (alternate views)

Ridgehand Block

TECHNIQUE

Ridgehand Block – Execution

APPLICATION

The ridgehand block utilizes the radial bone of the fore-arm as the blocking surface. The block covers a great range of motion and can be used to defend both low and high attacks. To perform the block, start the arm angled down-ward with the fingers pointed to the ground and the palm facing your body. Point the tip of the elbow at the target and sweep the blocking arm in a circular motion. When completed, the shoulder is dipped slightly and the elbow is bent at approximately a 90 degree angle with the knuckles in line with the eyes.

1. White attacks Black with a cross-side wrist grab. Black's arm and hand are in the starting position for a ridgehand block. White can use this attack to pull Black off balance, preventing him from mounting any type of counterattack.

2. Black sweeps his arm downward and clockwise which mimics the correct range of motion for a ridgehand block. This sweeping circular motion results in White being taken off balance allowing Black to counterattack.

Step 1 & 2 *Ridgehand Block*

X – Block

TECHNIQUE

X - Block – Execution

APPLICATION

Black uses the x-block to execute a cross choke on White. Black slides one hand, palm up, into the opposite side lapel of White, and performs the same action on the opposite side. Once both of Black's hands are secured inside of White's lapels and the bones of the forearms are pressed against the sides of White's neck, downward pressure is applied with the knee to White's abdominal area while Black's bends the ulnar sides of his wrists toward his forearms.

High Block

TECHNIQUE

High Block – Execution

APPLICATION

The high block is one of the most recognizable techniques in the martial arts. It is found in some variation in nearly every striking art and is often overlooked as a viable grappling tool. To perform a left high block, the practitioner crosses his left arm over at his waist to the opposite side in a coiling-type preparation. When executing the block, the hips are whipped back to the left side and the arm follows in an upward direction. Upon finishing, the fist is above the head, with the forearm angling downward approximately 45 degrees.

1. White attacks Black with a same-side shoulder grab. From this position, White can pull or push Black's shoulder, off-balancing him and gaining an advantage.

2. Black defends White's grabbing attack by attacking the hand that attacked him. Black uses the non-blocking hand to grab White's wrist and perform a wrist lock to take him off-balance. Black uses the blocking arm to push up against the underside of White's arm. The simultaneous pull-down/push-up motion of the arms creates a lever with White's elbow as the fulcrum.

Step 1 & 2 *High Block*

Outer Forearm Block

TECHNIQUE

Outer Forearm Block – Preparation   Outer Forearm Block – Execution

APPLICATION

The outer forearm block is a basic blocking technique that resembles the ridgehand block in its application except for the fact that it uses a closed fist rather than an open hand. It is so named because the outer surface of the forearm is used as the striking surface for the block. To prepare for this block, the arms are crossed over one another on the side of the body parallel to the ground at chest level with the blocking arm stacked on top. Once the preparation is complete, execution of the block requires the practitioner to snap the hips in the blocking direction allowing the arm to follow so that the blocking arm finishes with the elbow bent at a 90 degree angle, in line with the lead leg, with the fist at chin level.

1. To use the outer forearm block in a grappling situation, Black attacks White with a same-side wrist attack.

Black attacks in this manner to allow himself the ability to pull White off balance and control his movement. This control over movement is a staple of grappling and it allows Black to further attack White with the technique of his choice.

2. Black uses the wrist grabbing attack to pull White off balance. Black pulls White toward him by combining the pulling motion of his arms with the turning of his hips. Notice that Black uses his other (blocking) arm to further pull White off balance.

3. Black completes the arm-locking/off-balancing technique on White by continuing the hip-turning action. Black maintains his grip on White's sleeve near the wrist while driving the other arm into White's shoulder so that he maintains control over his movement.

Step 1 *Outer Forearm Block*

Step 2 *Outer Forearm Block*

Step 3 *Outer Forearm Block*

Inner Forearm Block

TECHNIQUE

Inner Forearm Block – Preparation   *Inner Forearm Block – Execution*

APPLICATION

The inner forearm block for many practitioners is a more powerful block than the outer forearm block due to the ease with which the hips may be used. It is so named because the inner surface of the forearm is used as the striking surface for the block. The inner forearm block differs from the outer in that the rear arm is used for this blocking technique. To prepare for the block, the practitioner chambers the blocking hand behind the ear with the elbow at a 90 degree angle and the fist at head level. Simultaneously, the front hand is extended to the front. To execute the block, the hips are turned in the direction of the lead hand and the blocking arm is brought in along a half circle in front of the body in a plane parallel to the ground.

1. White attacks Black with a same-side wrist attack. White attacks in the manner to allow himself the ability to pull Black off balance and control his movement. As previously mentioned, this control over movement is a staple of

grappling and it allows White to control the confrontation by allowing him to choose the technique of his choice while limiting Black's counterattack options.

2. Black uses the block preparation to off-balance White in his counterattack. Black does this by grabbing White's sleeve with his lead hand and pulling White's attacking arm into him with the chambering motion of the block. This combination of movement is important for two reasons: first it negates White's attempts to pull Black off balance; and second, it binds White's hands so that he is unable to use them to strike Black.

3. Black continues the pulling motion of the lead hand and combines it with the turning of his hips. This is done while the blocking hand moves from its chambered position to that which is used during the execution phase. This combination of movements completely disrupts White's balance allowing him to be pulled to the ground.

Step 1 *Inner Forearm Block*

Step 2 *Inner Forearm Block*

Step 3 *Inner Forearm Block*

Reverse Inner Forearm Block

TECHNIQUE

Reverse Inner Forearm Block – Preparation   *Reverse Inner Forearm Block – Execution*

APPLICATION

The reverse inner forearm block is so named for the direction it moves in relation to the traditional inner forearm block. This is an underutilized technique that is often overlooked outside of pattern training. The reason is simple; it is an awkward technique to use to block an incoming attack. The reverse inner forearm block does however have good grappling applications due to its use of the hips throughout its execution. To prepare for the block, the arms are crossed in much the same way as they were for the preparation of the outer forearm block. The only difference is that the arms are in front of the body for this block rather than to the side. To execute the block, the hips are snapped in the direction of the blocking arm with the arm finishing in the same position as that of the outer forearm block with the exception that the forearm is pronated rather than supinated.

1. White attacks Black with a cross-side wrist attack. By using this attack, White can not only disrupt Black's balance by pulling him forward, but more importantly, he can turn him so that Black's back will face White. Getting

the back of the opponent is a primary strategy for most grappling arts as it gives White easier access to choking and takedown techniques.

2. Black defends the grabbing attack by grabbing White's belt with his preparation hand and pulling White's attacking hand into his body as part of the execution of the block. Doing so allows Black to offset the leverage White gained through the grabbing attack and it puts Black in a better position to counterattack.

3. Black continues the circular motion of the block while pulling the preparation arm into his hip. Drawing the hand into the hip gives Black greater control over White and allows him to better control his movement. The blocking motion of the other arm serves in two ways: first, if White keeps his grip on Black's wrist, Black will be able to continue the circular motion into a joint lock; second, if White releases his grip throughout the course of Black's arm motion, Black is then free from the grabbing attack and is able to use the control he has over White's hips to counterattack with a striking technique.

Step 1 *Reverse Inner Forearm Block*

Step 2 *Reverse Inner Forearm Block*

Step 3 *Reverse Inner Forearm Block*

Twin Reverse Inner Forearm Block

TECHNIQUE

Twin Reverse Inner Forearm Block – Preparation   *Twin Reverse Inner Forearm Block – Execution*

APPLICATION

Much like the reverse inner forearm block, this block does not have many uses against true striking attacks. It does however have numerous grappling applications due to the spreading movement of the arms and the stable stance typically assumed during the technique. Preparation for the block requires the practitioner to cross their arms in front of the chest with the fists at the level of the collarbones. Execution of the block is performed by uncrossing the arms and moving them apart in a spreading motion so that they finish slightly further apart than shoulder-width. When in a finished position, the shoulders are nearly straight out to the sides and the elbows are bent at a 90 degree angle and held away from the body.

1. White attacks Black with a control technique called the "plum." By using this technique, White is able to manipulate where Black's head is able to go, thereby controlling where Black himself is able to go. From this position, White can utilize elbow and knee strikes as well as initiate takedown or throwing techniques. From this position, Black has no ability to control the course of the confrontation.

2. Black begins to defend against the plum by using the crossing his arms as is done in the preparation phase of the twin reverse inner forearm block. In doing this, Black is spreading White's elbows apart, which weakens the grip White has around his head and neck. This will give Black the space he needs to begin his escape from White's attack.

3. Black continues the spreading motion with his arms which further weakens White's grip around his head and neck. Notice the increase in the amount of space that has been made between Black and White as a result of the spreading motion of the block. This increase in space affords Black more mobility to escape or possibly counterattack.

Step 1 *Twin Reverse Inner Forearm Block*

Step 2 *Twin Reverse Inner Forearm Block*

Step 3 *Twin Reverse Inner Forearm Block*

Scooping Block

TECHNIQUE

Scooping Block – Preparation   *Scooping Block – Execution*

APPLICATION

The scooping block resembles the outer forearm block although it differs in application and use. The scooping block employs a circular motion similar to the outer forearm block, but the diameter of the circle it travels is greatly expanded. It is for this reason that the scooping block is often taught as a tool to block attacks to the body and legs while the outer forearm block is often used to defend against chest and head attacks. Preparation for the scooping block begins from a front stance with the blocking arm extended down the side of the body. Execution occurs when the practitioner snaps the hips and allows his arm to travel in a circle until the arm is at the side of the body with the elbow bent 90 degrees with the fist is at chin level.

1. Black utilizes the scooping block much like a wrestler's ankle pick technique. In this technique, Black drops to his knees while moving toward White, much like a wrestler's shot, and grabs the lead leg with one hand while using the scooping block to remove that leg from the ground.

Note that Black's hips are facing White as he is scooping the leg. Black will combine the ankle pull and the blocking motion on the back of the leg with his forward movement to throw White's center of gravity backward and off balance.

2. Black continues the forward pull on the leg and the blocking motion of the arm to further pull White off balance. Black has hooked his blocking arm completely under White's leg and will use that hook to pull White completely off balance. Black could take White to the ground at this point by kicking White's base leg or stepping in front of it while pulling on his leg. Black has many options, both striking and takedown, from this position.

3. Black has turned his hip into White's leg, thereby completely disrupting his balance making it easier to take him to the ground. Black now has control over White's left leg and is in a good position to strike White's groin to end the confrontation.

Step 1 *Scooping Block*

Step 2 *Scooping Block*

Step 3 *Scooping Block*

Hooking Block

TECHNIQUE

Hooking Block – Execution

APPLICATION

The hooking block is an underutilized technique in the Taekwondo arsenal. The hooking block is a useful tool in both the striking and grappling arenas. The preparation for the block is similar to the circular motion used for the ridgehand block with the arm traveling in a circular fashion from low to high. The only difference is that the hand is turned over at the top of the circle so that the hand is used in a grabbing fashion rather than using the ridgehand surface of the hand as the blocking implement.

1. White has attacked Black with a cross-side wrist grab which would enable him to pull Black off balance and control his movement. Upon being attacked in this manner, Black immediately steps off the line of attack and begins to swing his arm in the direction of his movement.

2. Black has continued his movement off the line of attack while continuing the arm swing of the hooking block. By doing so, he has turned the tables and taken White off balance instead. From this improved position and through control of White's arm, Black has the ability to release his grip and escape or deliver a round kick to White's face, abdomen, or legs.

Step 1 *Hooking Block*

Step 2 *Hooking Block*

Pole/U-Shaped Block

TECHNIQUE

Pole/U-Shaped Block – Execution

APPLICATION

The pole or u-shaped block is often taught as a defense against a strike with a staff or even as a striking technique to the throat and groin. It does not lend itself very well to blocking incoming striking attacks as it is a slow block that does not seem to move at any angle to be useful. It does, however, have a grappling application that is useful for the downed Taekwondo practitioner. The block is performed by chambering the hands at the hips and thrusting them forward into the position seen to the left.

Below you see that Black has been knocked to the ground by White. By trapping White's foot, Black is able to push him off balance by using his top hand to apply pressure to White's hip. This simultaneous push/pull motion will force White to stop his attack to recover his balance or to fall to the ground.

Pole/U-Shaped Block

Twin Palm Block

TECHNIQUE

Twin Palm Block – Execution

APPLICATION

The twin palm block is an uncommon open hand block seen in the color belt pattern Hwarang. Like many other twin blocking techniques, it is not effective for defense as it is difficult to execute it with any speed. Furthermore, the positioning of the hands makes it essentially useless for blocking any attacks of substance. However, the twisting motion of the wrists during this technique gives it excellent grappling applications that may be utilized to advance a counterattacking technique.

1. White attacks Black with a twin wrist grabbing technique. This is an effective attack for White as he can use it to negate most of Black's movement, and it gives him the ability to control Black's ability to strike him with hand or foot strikes.

2. Black utilizes the outward circular motion of the wrists during the twin palm block to begin to free himself from White's grip. Black is successful in breaking White's grasp as he is attacking White's thumbs, which are the weakest part of the grip.

3. Black has completed the circular motion of the twin palm block and by grabbing White's fingers, has reversed the grabbing attack into a twin wrist lock. From this position, Black can increase the intensity of the pain he inflicts on White, thereby controlling him and making it easier for him to move White where he wants him to go.

Step 1 *Twin Palm Block*

Step 2 *Twin Palm Block*

Step 3 *Twin Palm Block*

Scissor Block

TECHNIQUE

Scissor Block – Preparation   *Scissor Block – Execution*

APPLICATION

The scissor block is a seemingly odd-looking technique performed in the black belt Po-Eun pattern, as well as a few others. While it does seem to have a feasible application, such as a defense against simultaneous punching and kicking or double kicking attacks, the scissoring movement of the block makes it an excellent grappling technique that utilizes its natural leverage. The preparation and execution phases of the scissor block are the same. Preparation for a right hand high scissor block involves assuming the left hand high scissor block position and then switching arm position for the execution phase.

1. Black is attempting to utilize the scissor block on White in the form of a throwing technique. In order to see the grappling application of the scissor block, you must change the plane in which the technique occurs. While the blocking technique occurs in a vertical plane, the grappling application occurs in a horizontal one. Black lowers his center of gravity below White's and creates a fulcrum at White's hips by placing one arm behind White's knees and

the other across his abdomen. Note that Black bends his legs to lower himself into a position to throw White instead of simply bending at the waist.

2. Black uses his leg and hip posture from the initial position to create force for the technique. Black drives upward while scissoring his arms to lift White off the ground. Notice that Black's initial position allows him to be in a stable position while he controls White's body off of the ground. Black does not simply pick White up off the ground; rather he combines his upward drive and the scissoring action of the block to lift White. This combination of movement makes the lifting portion of the throw effortless. From this position, the end result is obvious; Black will either drop or drive White onto his back or head.

3. Black has dropped White onto his back. Black can either escape by releasing White's leg or he can control White's position by driving his knee into White's chest and proceed to finish him with strikes.

Step 1 *Scissor Block*

Step 2 *Scissor Block*

Step 3 *Scissor Block*

Double Knifehand Block

TECHNIQUE

Double Knifehand Block – Preparation

Double Knifehand Block – Execution

APPLICATION

The double knifehand block is one of the more recognizable blocking techniques in Taekwondo's arsenal. It is another in a series of blocking technique that while useful in an abbreviated form to defend against strikes, performing the block in the proper fashion requires too much time for it to be a viable defensive tool. While its grappling application is hidden, the combined hip and arm action required for this technique gives it useful grappling applications. Preparation requires the practitioner to rotate their hips to the rear as they extend their arms behind their bodies while keeping them parallel to the ground. The practitioner executes the block by rapidly rotating their hips to the front which leads to a whipping motion of the arms and the conclusion of the block. The finishing position finds the blocking arm held just below shoulder level with the elbow bent at a 90 degree angle. The opposite hand is held palm up at chest level with the elbow pointing to the rear.

1. Black begins the application of the double knifehand block by grabbing White's lapel with his right hand and his wrist with the blocking arm. The back or L-stance typically employed with the double knifehand block puts Black in a stable position to perform the technique.

2. Black begins the forward motion of the knifehand while maintaining his grip on White's lapel and wrist. Simultaneously, Black widens his stance so that his hips are blocking those of White so that they will serve as a fulcrum for the throwing technique. The blocking of White's hips by Black is crucial to this technique and underscores the need for strong stances in Taekwondo training. It is important to note that as Black lowers his hips below White's, it allows him to load White onto his hip, disrupting his balance and makes the technique possible.

3. Black continues the forward hip motion of the block which has fully disrupted White's balance and taken him off of his feet. It is because of Black's hip position below White's that Black is able to easily take White off the ground and over his hips.

4. With the hip and arm motion complete, Black has thrown White over his hips to the ground. While it may appear hidden, the principles behind a proper double knifehand block are quite similar to those of a hip throw technique.

Step 1 *Double Knifehand Block*

Step 2 *Double Knifehand Block*

Step 3 *Double Knifehand Block*

Step 4 *Double Knifehand Block*

Low Double Knifehand Block

TECHNIQUE

Low Double Knifehand Block – Preparation   *Low Double Knifehand Block – Execution*

APPLICATION

The low double knifehand block is quite similar to the previously discussed double knifehand block. The primary difference between the two is that while the double knifehand block is traditionally employed to defend against hand strikes to the face, the low double knifehand block is used to defend against kicking attacks like the front or round kick. The preparation for the low double knifehand block is identical to that of the double knifehand block. The hips are turned toward the rear and the arms are extended behind the body while parallel to the ground. The execution of the low double knifehand block is similar to that of its upright cousin. The exception being that the low double knifehand block has the arms angled at a 45 degree angle with the fingers pointing to the ground, rather than kept parallel to the ground.

1. White attacks Black with a cross-side wrist grab. This technique allows White to control Black's movement to the front and the rear and it also gives White the ability to turn Black and take his back to apply choking and takedown techniques.

2. Black begins the chamber of the block by turning his hips to the rear to put him in a position to use his hips for a powerful counterattack. In turning his hips, Black brings White's attacking arm across his body and into the power of Black's hips. Black grabs White's attacking wrist as the arms reach their full extension.

3. Black begins to rotate his hips the opposite way in the direction of the block and uses his grip on White's wrist with his blocking hand as a joint-locking technique to control White's movement and lead him into his counterattack. Notice that the opposite hand gives Black greater control by controlling White's head and neck.

4. Black continues to rotate his hips and continue his arm motion to the front further disrupting White's balance to the point where he will be forced to the ground. It is important to note that throughout the hip action of the blocking technique, Black's hands keep their grip on White's wrist and the back of his head/neck for controlling purposes.

After the completion of the hip rotation and arm movement, White has been taken to the ground as a result of the joint lock and is still being controlled by Black who is now in a superior position with control over his movement. From this position, Black is capable of counterattacks to his downed opponent, he can increase the pressure on the joint lock, or he can simply release the lock and escape.

Step 1 *Low Double Knifehand Block*

Step 2 *Low Double Knifehand Block*

Step 3 *Low Double Knifehand Block*

Step 4 *Low Double Knifehand Block*

Twin Downward Block

TECHNIQUE

Twin Downward Block – Preparation   *Twin Downward Block – Execution*

APPLICATION

The twin downward block is like many other blocks in that it does not have an obvious application for defense against a striking attack. The twin downward block does, however, have a useful grappling tool for controlling an opponent's position, specifically for pulling an opponent to the ground. The reason for this is the dropping of the body weight during the execution of the block. The practitioner prepares for the block by crossing the arms in front of the body at chest level, much like the preparation position for the twin reverse inner forearm block. Execution occurs when the arms are uncrossed and thrust downward so that the ending position is just above the thighs with the arms slightly rounded.

1. Black assumes the preparation position of the twin downward block by using the fist position of the hands as a crossed grabbing attack to White's lapel. Black's hands are crossed and positioned inside the lapel so that they can be used to control White by the lapel or they may be easily moved up the collar onto the neck so that the bones of the forearms are against the sides of White's neck with Black's thumbs able to touch the back of White's neck.

2. Black executes the choking technique by stepping backward and dropping his weight. The weight dropping causes White to be pulled forward and downward and therefore off balance. When Black drops his weight and pulls White down, Black's grip on White's lapel tightens resulting in a choking technique with the bones of Black's forearms pressing against White's carotid arteries.

Step 1 *Twin Downward Block*

Step 2 *Twin Downward Block*

Twin Outer Forearm Block

TECHNIQUE

Twin Outer Forearm Block – Preparation   *Twin Outer Forearm Block – Execution*

APPLICATION

The twin outer forearm block, like most double blocks, has more grappling applications than striking applications. Preparation for this block involves crossing the arms in front of the body, much like that which was done for the twin downward block, except that the arms are parallel, rather than perpendicular, to the ground. Execution is performed by circling the arms upward and outward in a circular motion.

1. White attacks Black by attempting to grab his legs. If White is allowed to continue unchecked, he will grab one or both of Black's legs, control his hips, lift him up and drive him into the ground. The shot takedown will likely give White complete control over the altercation leaving Black unable to utilize any of his striking tools.

2. Black begins to defend against the leg grab by moving his hips and legs away from White in a technique that is a

modification of a wrestler's sprawl. Black is also moving his arms in the preparation position for the twin outer forearm block so that he will eventually gain control over White's upper body, thereby slowing the execution of White's shot takedown attempt.

3. Black performs the execution phase of the twin outer forearm block on White and has achieved control of White's body by securing double underhooks. Note that Black has also moved his hips and legs away from White, thereby preventing him from completing his attack. Because Black has maintained his stability, he is now able to counterattack White's takedown attempt by kneeing him in the mid-section, or by stepping in a circular motion with his rear leg and lifting with his right arm, Black would be able to throw White to the ground.

Step 1 *Twin Outer Forearm Block*

Step 2 *Twin Outer Forearm Block*

Step 3 *Twin Outer Forearm Block*

Mountain Block

TECHNIQUE

Mountain Block – Preparation   *Mountain Block – Execution*

APPLICATION

The mountain block is one of the more aesthetically pleasing blocks in the Taekwondo practitioner's arsenal. While technically the block is designed to defend against simultaneous side attacks; it is the hip action and weight dropping that occurs during the course of the block that gives it its grappling application. Black prepares for the block by crossing his arms in front of his body while in a back stance. Execution occurs when Black snaps his hips and lowers his weight into a sitting stance which allows the arms to move to their finishing position.

1. Black has utilized the weight dropping portion of the technique to assume a position lower than that of White. Black's left arm controls White's right arm and Black's right arm is in a position to control White's hips. Note that Black has moved himself below White's center of gravity by bending his knees and lowering himself to the ground, not bending his back.

2. Black has employed the hip turn of the mountain block combined with the pulling of White's arm and the lifting of his hips to break his balance and lift him off of the ground. From this position, it becomes obvious that the mountain block application is a kneeling kata guruma or shoulder wheel judo throw or a wrestler's fireman's carry takedown. As Black has completely taken White's balance, he will continue the circular motion of the throw by pulling down on White's arm while lifting up on his thigh. This combination of movements will allow Black to throw White over his shoulders and onto the mat.

3. Black has finished the takedown and is now in a position of control over White. By controlling his leg and arm, Black has many options on how to proceed. Black can pivot across White's body and apply a kneebar or he can perform an armbar on White's outstretched arm. Lastly, Black has the ability to strike White in numerous targets.

Step 1 *Mountain Block*

Step 2 *Mountain Block*

Step 3 *Mountain Block*

CHAPTER
3

Grappling in Strikes and Kicks

Lunge Punch

TECHNIQUE

Lunge Punch – Execution

APPLICATION

The lunge punch is probably the first striking technique learned in the traditional martial arts that focus on striking. While the technique may seem to be one that has no use outside of striking, it is the attributes that make it a powerful striking technique that also give it its grappling application. The power of the lunge punch comes from the simultaneous forward momentum of the body and the snapping of the hips into the punch. The retraction of the non-punching hand back to the hip adds to the power of the strike.

1. Black sets up the grappling application of the lunge punch by attacking White with a double grabbing technique. In doing so, Black controls both sides of White's body and is able to manipulate his center of gravity and pull him off balance into either strikes or takedown techniques.

2. Black utilizes the leverage from his grabbing attack to perform the grappling application of the lunge punch on White. Black uses the simultaneous push/pull motion of the lunge punch to pull White's right arm while pushing his left arm so that White is thrown off balance. Because Black combined his hip movement with the arm movement, he is now in a position to execute a powerful round kick into White's legs or back. Alternately, if Black desires, he can continue the push/pull motion and drive White to the ground.

Step 1
Lunge Punch

Step 2 *Lunge Punch*

Reverse Punch

TECHNIQUE

Reverse Punch – Execution

APPLICATION

The reverse punch is performed in much the same way as the lunge punch. The push/pull action of the arms combined with the snapping motion of the hips provides the strike with a great deal of power. The primary difference between the two techniques is the leg placement in relation to the striking hand. In the reverse punch, the striking arm and the opposite leg are forward, unlike the lunge punch where same arm and leg are forward.

1. Black attacks White with a lapel/hip grab combination. Black's hand position is a common one in many grappling arts as it allows Black to control White at two pivot points of his body, the shoulders and the hips. With the grip, Black is able to control White's position and move wherever he needs.

2. Black uses the push/pull motion of the reverse punch by pushing with the shoulder grip and simultaneously pulling with the hip grip. This allows Black to force White into an off-balanced position. Note the position of Black's lead leg as he combines the arm action with a foot-tripping technique to ensure that White will be unable to regain his balance.

Step 1 *Reverse Punch*

Step 2 *Reverse Punch*

Hook Punch

TECHNIQUE

Hook Punch – Execution

APPLICATION

The Taekwondo hook punch is quite similar to the boxing punch of the same name. It is the difference in its execution that gives the boxing version the advantage. In Taekwondo, most punching techniques are seldom used as anything other than a set up for kicking techniques. Because of this, the Taekwondo punch is typically executed without the hip action needed for it to be a formidable offensive striking technique. Its circular nature does, however, give it a useful grappling application.

1. Black uses the hook punch on White as an attack from the back. Black uses his left hand to prevent White from turning and uses the hook punch by locating it close to the jaw line to set up a controlling technique. By controlling White's shoulder and head, Black has control over White's mobility and stability.

2. Black continues the hook punch technique utilizing it as a control technique on White's head and neck. Note the change in Black's hip position from Step 1 to Step 2. It is through the turning of the hips that Black derives the power to gain firm control over White's head and neck. From this position, Black may either continue turning or drag White to the ground, or Black may fully turn his hips and use his grip on White's head as leverage to throw him over his hips.

Step 1 *Hook Punch*   **Step 2** *Hook Punch*

Palm Strike

TECHNIQUE

Palm Strike – Execution

APPLICATION

The palm strike is performed with similar mechanics to the lunge punch. However, the differences in grappling application are as different as the physical appearance of the individual techniques. Whereas the lunge punch (or any fist strike) may be applied as a grabbing attack, the palm strike is interpreted as a pushing technique that is used to allow the practitioner to create space between himself and his attacker.

1. White attacks Black with a frontal throat grab. This is a useful attack in that it gives White the ability to control Black's head and therefore his balance. White can use this attack to drive Black backwards into a wall or other inescapable position or White can simply squeeze Black's neck, effectively choking him and possibly damaging Black's trachea.

2. Black defends against White's throat grab by attacking the weak point of the one-handed grab—the thumb; by turning in the direction of the thumb, Black weakens White's grip. Black facilitates the escape by turning his hips away from the attack while striking White in the ribs with his palm strike. The effectiveness of the palm strike to the ribs is twofold: first, it weakens White by striking him in a sensitive area; and two, it creates a wedge that helps to separate Black from White's grip. From this position, Black can either escape or capitalize on White's momentary weakness and follow-up with a striking counterattack.

Step 1 *Palm Strike*

Step 2 *Palm Strike*

Knifehand Strike

TECHNIQUE

Knifehand Strike – Preparation

Knifehand Strike – Execution

APPLICATION

The knifehand strike is one of the most well-known strikes found in traditional martial arts. To execute a knifehand strike, the arms are crossed and the striking hand is chambered on top of the other arm. The power in the strike comes from the snapping motion of the hip that results in the knifehand moving on a plane parallel to the ground.

1. Black attacks White with a cross-side lapel grab. By using this technique, Black will be able to pull White off balance making his striking technique more effective and powerful.

2. Black pulls the arm used to grab White across his body and assumes the chamber position for the knifehand strike. In doing so, he pulls White off balance and opens up potential targets for his knifehand strike.

3. Black continues the pulling motion and as he does so, he opens his hips with a snapping motion toward White. This allows the knifehand strike to contact White with a whipping motion thereby increasing the power of the strike. Depending on the relative proximity between Black and White, the elbow, forearm, or knifehand will be the striking implement. Note the position of Black's lead foot in relation to White's lead foot.

4. Black continues the knifehand strike while simultaneously sweeping White's lead leg out from underneath him, effectively disrupting his balance. The combined push/pull of the knifehand strike/leg sweep combination allows Black to take White to the ground, allowing Black to safely escape or counterattack to end the confrontation.

Step 1 *Knifehand Strike*

Step 2 *Knifehand Strike*

Step 3 *Knifehand Strike*

Step 4 *Knifehand Strike*

Twin Knifehand Strike

TECHNIQUE

Twin Knifehand Strike – Preparation

Twin Knifehand Strike – Execution

APPLICATION

The twin knifehand strike is another of the Taekwondo hand techniques that does not seem to have a viable practical application. It does not tend to be a practical strike due its lack of speed in execution as well as it taking unlikely circumstances to be an appropriate tool to use to defend oneself. However, the twin knifehand strike does build shoulder and arm strength in the practitioner and teaches them to be aware of symmetry of position. Preparation of the twin knifehand involves crossing the arms in front of the body much like the single knifehand attack. Upon execution, the practitioner rapidly extends both arms in opposite directions while keeping each arm parallel to the floor.

1. White attacks Black with a double hand lapel grab. With this attack, White has the ability to begin to attack Black's balance. White is now in a position to push or pull Black in any direction he feels necessary.

2. Black begins to defend against White's attack by assuming the preparation position for the twin knife-

hand strike. Black's palms are facing him so that when he executes the techniques, the twisting of his forearms to a palms away position will serve to further loosen White's grip. Furthermore, Black has now made contact with White's arms so he can now feel White's movements and adjust to them easier.

3. Black has moved into the execution phase of the twin knifehand strike and in doing so has completely broken White's hold on him. Additionally, Black has combined the twin knifehand movement with a backward step to increase the prying power of the technique. Also note that the twin knifehand strike applies pressure to White's grip in such a way that it attacks White's thumbs, which are the weakest part of the grip. From this position, Black may now perform a counterattack against White's grab by grabbing him behind the head and driving a knee strike into White's abdomen, or Black may simply choose to escape.

Step 1 *Twin Knifehand Strike*

Step 2 *Twin Knifehand Strike*

Step 3 *Twin Knifehand Strike*

Spearhand Strike

TECHNIQUE

Spearhand Strike – Execution

APPLICATION

The spearhand is a striking technique unique to the martial arts. With the striking surface consisting of tips of the fingers, it has found its niche as a board breaking technique for demonstrations with very little practical application. It is often taught that its application in patterns is that of a block with the supporting hand followed by the spearhand to the solar plexus of the attacker. While striking the solar plexus with the tips of the fingers would be effective, it would be too difficult to perform in a real situation and furthermore, a reverse punch would be more effective. The spearhand is performed in much the same way as the reverse punch, complete with the opposite hand foot combination and snapping of the hips for power.

1. White attacks Black with a basic lapel grab. By using this technique, White will be able to pull Black off balance making his own subsequent striking technique more effective and powerful. However, Black is not helpless in this position as he is able to attack White just as easily. White's grabbing attack only gives him an advantage if he follows it quickly with another offensive attack.

2. Black begins the preparation for the striking by using the supporting hand to trap White's hand to his chest. From this position, Black has the ability to execute a joint lock or to begin to control White's arm, leading into a counterattack.

3. With White's hand trapped, Black executes the spearhand strike underneath White's attacking arm. By thrusting the spearhand under White's arm between the shoulder and the elbow, Black effectively locks out both White's shoulder and elbow. Black can continue thrusting the spearhand forward to further disrupt White's balance, he can continue into a wrist lock with the left hand, or he can simply use White's unbalanced position to begin striking him.

Step 1 *Spearhand Strike*

Step 2 *Spearhand Strike*

Step 3 *Spearhand Strike*

Ridgehand Strike

TECHNIQUE

Ridgehand Strike – Execution

APPLICATION

The ridgehand strike is one of the more unorthodox techniques found in Taekwondo, both in appearance and application. The striking surface of the ridgehand or reverse knifehand as it is sometimes called is the fleshy area between the thumb and index finger. The ridgehand is not often used in sparring as the circular path it travels makes it slower than most other hand techniques. It is however that circular path that makes it a fine tool for breaking demonstrations as well as grappling.

1. White attacks Black with a looping punch, which is a technique often employed by unskilled fighters. Black evades the punch by stepping off the line of attack at a 45 degree angle and begins the circular motion of the ridgehand strike.

2. Black continues the circular ridgehand motion while avoiding the looping punch, which results in Black achieving a position on White's side with White's arm trapped to prevent him from striking with it again. The ridgehand strike impacts White's chest/neck and will disorient him for a time.

3. Black continues his movement allowing his momentum and the momentum of White's strike to pull him to White's back. Black allows the circular nature of the ridgehand strike to continue around White's neck leading to a single wing choke. From this rear position, Black is safe from White's strikes and is able to escape or counterattack unimpeded.

Step 1 *Ridgehand Strike*

Step 2 *Ridgehand Strike*

Step 3 *Ridgehand Strike*

Twin High Punch

TECHNIQUE

Twin High Punch – Execution

APPLICATION

The twin high punch is a striking technique often used to teach symmetry of motion and coordination within a Taekwondo pattern. It is not a highly successful sparring technique due to its slower speed and lack of adaptability. Its symmetry does however give it a useful grappling application.

1. Black uses the twin fists of the high punch as grabbing attacks and secures his grip on White's lapels. Black is in a position to strike White with his knees or to release his grip with one hand and execute an elbow strike.

2. From the lapel grab position, Black drives his fists into the sides of White's neck (carotid arteries) eliciting a choking technique. Black is now controlling White's movement and with that control has the ability to sweep White to the ground and continue the choking technique there.

Step 1 *Twin High Punch*   **Step 2** *Twin High Punch*

Rear High Elbow Strike

TECHNIQUE

Rear High Elbow Strike – Execution

APPLICATION

The rear high elbow strike is one of the many elbow strikes used in Taekwondo. The rear high elbow strike (like the rear low elbow strike) is most often used in self-defense situations to disable an attacker from the rear before beginning a counterattack of strikes, joint locks, or to simply escape. Its execution is quite simple with the only parameter being that the striking arm remains parallel to the ground.

The grappling application of the rear high elbow strike is not as overt as it is for other striking techniques. This elbow strike is primarily utilized to pull the opponent into position for some other striking or grappling counterattack.

1. Black prepares for the elbow strike by reaching forward and grabbing White by the lapel. This grip allows Black the opportunity to work for a higher level of control over White, which could lead to greater force in his striking and grappling attacks.

2. Black executes the rear high elbow strike and the result is White being pulled forward and off balance. Note the action of Black's hips as he executes the elbow strike. By stepping back and powering the movement with his hips, Black has a better ability to pull White off balance. Simply pulling with the arm will not provide sufficient force to elicit the desired effect.

Step 1 *Rear High Elbow Strike*

Step 2 *Rear High Elbow Strike*

Twin Rear High Elbow

TECHNIQUE

Twin Rear High Elbow – Execution

APPLICATION

The twin rear high elbow strike does not typically have the usefulness in self defense situations that a single elbow strike would possess for a couple of reasons. First, the use of both arms simultaneously negates the ability of the practitioner to utilize their hips most effectively. Second, self-defense situations in which the attackers are positioned symmetrically around their prey are rare at best. The technique is performed the same way as the rear high elbow strike, except for the fact that both elbows are thrust to the rear simultaneously. The mechanics of the twin rear high elbow strike make it a powerful choking technique.

1. Black attacks White from the rear with a cross lapel grab.

2. By executing the elbow strike, Black's grip on White's gi pulls the lapels across the throat resulting in a rear cross choke technique.

Step 2 *Twin Rear High Elbow*

Step 1 *Twin Rear High Elbow*

Upward Vertical Elbow Strike

TECHNIQUE

Upward Vertical Elbow Strike – Execution

APPLICATION

Elbows are often forgotten weapons within the striking arsenal of Taekwondo. This is due to the fact that elbow strikes have no place in the rules of Taekwondo sparring and are typically only utilized in patterns and breaking. Understanding the grappling applications of elbow strikes will allow you to use them as something other than close-quarter strikes. To perform an upward vertical elbow strike, simply flex the elbow as much as possible and swing the bent arm upward so that the point of the elbow moves upward from the floor to the ceiling.

1. White attacks Black with a same-side shoulder grab. This attacking technique may be used to off-balance Black for a takedown, to turn him to take his back to apply a choke, or to stabilize him for a kicking or punching attack.

2. Black traps White's hand and moves off the line of attack. Black then delivers an upward vertical elbow strike to White's elbow. From this position, Black has the ability to apply constant upward pressure on White's elbow, hyper-extending the joint, and thereby allowing him to control White and set up other strikes. Or, if Black so chooses, he can strike the elbow forcefully, breaking the joint and ending White's ability to fight.

Step 1 *Upward Vertical Elbow Strike*

Step 2 *Upward Vertical Elbow Strike*

Chon-Ji

Chon-Ji is the first pattern learned by the white belt Taekwondo practitioner. The word Chon-Ji translates to "Heaven and Earth." In Asian culture, it is interpreted as the creation of the universe and therefore should be the first pattern learned by the beginning student. This theme arises from the I Ching or "Book of Changes." It teaches the student the basic blocks and strikes of the style, including the downward block, which represents the earth, the outer forearm block, which represents heaven, and the lunge punch.

The four-directional movement of the pattern represents the four elements of heaven and earth: fire, water, earth, and spirit. Additionally, it teaches the student basic stepping and turning patterns as well as the concepts of shifting and dropping their weight. It also gives the student a basic understanding of loading an opponent's weight. It is through an understanding of shifting, dropping, and loading weight that a student can understand the concepts of keeping balance and off-balancing an opponent.

Lunge Punch to Downward Block

TECHNIQUE

Combination 1 – Lunge Punch to Downward Block

APPLICATION

1. Black uses the downward block as a grabbing technique. Notice how the center of gravity is kept between the feet and he is in a stable position.

2. Black completes the 180° turn. While doing so, Black is keeping his weight centered between his feet and keeping his knees bent. Notice that Black's belt is below that of White. This will allow Black to load White onto his back to complete the technique. If Black rises up out of the front stance he will not be able to off-balance White.

3. Black continues his turning motion and in doing so off-balances White so that he is pulled off the ground. This movement is possible because Black is keeping his center of gravity low and using his hips and body weight to move White.

4. Black finishes the motion by simultaneously stepping back with his left foot and pulling White over his shoulder. By dropping his weight and pulling White's arm, Black is able to throw White over his back and onto the mat.

Step 1 *Lunge Punch to Downward Block*

Step 2 *Lunge Punch to Downward Block*

Step 3 *Lunge Punch to Downward Block*

Step 4 *Lunge Punch to Downward Block*

Downward Block to Lunge Punch to Downward Block

TECHNIQUE

Combination 2 – Downward Block to Lunge Punch to Downward Block

APPLICATION

1. From a side-grabbing attack, Black will turn to face the attack by White. From this position, White is in an advantageous position as he has all of his weapons available with which to strike Black.

2. Black has turned to face White. In doing so, he has grabbed White's wrist while executing the downward block. The hip action utilized in the downward block transfers to Black's grabbing arm which allows him to pull White off balance.

3. By taking advantage of his superior position over White, Black continues to drop his weight to the ground.

While dropping to the ground, Black reaches around White's legs, locking his own arms, preventing White from getting away from him while controlling his balance.

4. Black utilizes the pivoting movement of the combination to further take White off balance. If Black were to continue moving into White as seen in the previous picture, White might have been able to step back and regain his balance. However, by pivoting on his knees and pulling with his hips, Black prevents this counterattack and takes White to the mat.

Step 1 *Downward Block to Lunge Punch To Downward Block*

Step 2 *Downward Block to Lunge Punch To Downward Block*

Step 3 *Downward Block to Lunge Punch To Downward Block*

Step 4 *Downward Block to Lunge Punch To Downward Block*

Downward Block to Lunge Punch

TECHNIQUE

Combination 3 – Downward Block to Lunge Punch

APPLICATION

1. Black attacks White by grabbing his wrist. This attack can be used to initiate striking attacks with the hands or feet or it can be used to pull White off balance.

2. Black uses his punching attack as an elbow locking technique on White. By using the fist strike as a grab to White's gi, Black creates a lever over which he can pull White's elbow with his chambering hand. From this position, Black can continue to lock the elbow, or he can take advantage of White's off-balanced position to turn into him and complete a shoulder throw.

Step 1 *Downward Block to Lunge Punch*

Step 2 *Downward Block to Lunge Punch*

Step 1 *Downward Block to Lunge Punch*
(Alternate View)

Step 2 *Downward Block to Lunge Punch (Alternate View)*

Lunge Punch to Outer Forearm Block

TECHNIQUE

Combination 4 – Lunge Punch to Outer Forearm Block

APPLICATION

1. Black uses the lunge punch in this application as a grabbing attack to White's forearm. By controlling White's forearm in this manner, Black is limiting the weapons that White can use against him as well as getting a feel for White's potential movements leading to a counterattack.

2. Black uses the chambering motion of the outer forearm block to take White off balance. Black then executes the outer forearm block as an elbow locking technique to White's arm. By pulling his right arm to his hip and following through with the block, Black is able to impart a great deal of force on White's shoulder. Black is now in a position to finish the altercation with a kicking attack to White's vulnerable front or rear.

Step 1 *Lunge Punch to Outer Forearm Block*

Step 2 *Lunge Punch to Outer Forearm Block*

Lunge Punch to Lunge Punch

TECHNIQUE

Combination 5 – Lunge Punch to Lunge Punch

APPLICATION

1. In this series, Black has completed a lunge punch and is grabbed from the rear by White. White is in a good position to pull Black off balance to the ground or strike him in the head, spine, ribs, or legs.

2. As Black steps backward into position for the second lunge punch, he drops his weight to get his center of gravity below White's. Black uses the pull/push motion of the lunge punch to load White's weight onto his hips in preparation for the throw.

3. As Black continues to drop his weight, White is further off-balanced and taken off of the ground. Black continues the push/pull motion with the arms in combination with lowering his weight to continue throwing White.

4. Black has completed the motion required to throw White and is in a position to execute his lunge punch. By keeping his hips below White's, Black was able to execute a shoulder throw by stepping backward into White, thereby off-balancing him enough to perform the throw.

Step 1 *Lunge Punch to Lunge Punch*

Step 2 *Lunge Punch to Lunge Punch*

Step 3 *Lunge Punch to Lunge Punch*

Step 4 *Lunge Punch to Lunge Punch*

Dan-Gun

The Dan-Gun pattern is learned by the yellow belt Taekwondo practitioner. In order to learn the meaning of the pattern, the practitioner must learn a little about Korean history. It is believed that early Manchurian, Chinese, and Mongolian people migrated to the area of present-day Korea to form the Chosun or "Land of the Morning Calm." It is from the name Chosun that the name Korea is derived. Dan-Gun is recognized as the leader of these people and the founder of Korea in 2333 B.C. The legend of Dan-Gun was said to have been created by the Bear Totem people and was brought back to life to develop a sense of national pride in the Korean people as a way to battle against invasion from the Chinese, Japanese, and Mongolian people. The Dan-Gun pattern teaches the student their first open-hand blocking and striking techniques, the double knifehand block and knifehand strike, respectively. It also introduces the student to the "I" or "H" shape stepping outline found in many Taekwondo patterns. Dan-Gun further emphasizes the weight dropping and turning skills introduced in Chon-ji and adds multiplanar attacks such as the circular knifehand strike followed by the straight line lunge punch). Lastly, Dan-Gun requires the student to begin to improve their coordination through the implementation of double-hand blocking techniques such as the double knifehand and square blocks.

Double Knifehand Block to High Punch

TECHNIQUE

Combination 1 – Double Knifehand Block to High Punch

APPLICATION

1. Black attacks White with a cross-side wrist grab. This technique in and of itself does not give Black all that much of an advantage over White, but it does allow him to gain control over one of White's weapon as well as giving Black the ability to take White off balance.

2. Black begins the chambering motion of the double knifehand block. In doing so, his hip turn allows him to pull White into him and somewhat off balance as is seen by White's weight being shifted onto his front foot. Notice that Black's forward hand (left) is in a position to strike White if the need arises.

3. Black uses the execution of the double knifehand block to simultaneously strike White in the chest/throat region with his knifehand while at the same time extended White's arm into a standing elbow lock. The power for this technique comes from the snapping of Black's hips into the technique, which has allowed him to push White backward onto his rear foot and even further off balance.

4. Black begins the high punch portion of the combination by grabbing White's lapel. Note that Black has slipped under White's arm after locking it in the previous photo. With Black now on the outside of White's body, he is relatively safe from striking attacks and is now in a position to completely disrupt White's balance. White, on the other hand, is now in no position to attempt any effective counterattack on Black.

5. Black continues the high punch motion by utilizing the stepping of the lunge punch to move behind White and take him further off balance. Note that Black's stepping motion ends with his foot just behind White's. This position prevents White from stepping backward to regain his balance, thereby stopping the takedown technique. Black finishes by using his hips as a fulcrum around which he can bring White to the ground with either a takedown or throwing technique.

Step 1 *Double Knifehand Block to High Punch*

Step 2 *Double Knifehand Block to High Punch*

Step 3 *Double Knifehand Block to High Punch*

Step 4 *Double Knifehand Block to High Punch*

Step 5 *Double Knifehand Block to High Punch*

High Punch to Double Knifehand Block to High Punch

TECHNIQUE

Combination 2 – High Punch to Double Knifehand Block to High Punch

APPLICATION

1. White attempts to strike Black with a basic jabbing attack. Black defends against this attack by using the footwork of the lunge punch to slip the jab and position himself to the outside of White's body. At the same time, Black utilizes the high punch as a grabbing attack to White's lapel/collar, giving him some control over White's ability to move.

2. Black uses the 180° turn of the pattern to position himself behind White, thereby eliminating most, if not all, of White's ability to counterattack. Black has also used the hip action of the turning motion to simultaneously get to White's back and tighten the grip he has on White's lapel, thereby increasing the pressure on White's throat. Note that

Black's finishing position after the turn is that of a double knifehand block.

3. Black finishes the combination by executing the lunge punch which, when done simultaneously with the lapel grab, results in a choking technique. By pulling White backward with the right hand he takes White's balance and uses White's body weight to tighten the lapel around his neck. When this downward and backward motion of White's body is combined with the forward motion of Black's punching attack, the choke becomes tight and gives Black an excellent amount of control over White.

Step 1 *High Punch to Double Knifehand Block to High Punch*

Step 2 *High Punch to Double Knifehand Block to High Punch*

Step 3 *High Punch to Double Knifehand Block to High Punch*

High Punch to Square Block

TECHNIQUE

Combination 3 – High Punch to Square Block

APPLICATION

1. White attacks Black with a cross punch attack. Black must evade this striking attack as the right cross is one of the stronger punching attacks that White could use. Black uses the right high punch as a grab to White's lapel with a simultaneous evasive movement to the outside of White's body. From this position, Black is able to avoid the majority of White's weapons while putting himself in a good position to counterattack.

2. Black uses the 270° turning motion during the transition from strike to block to take White's balance and load him onto his hip. The square block is utilized as a grabbing attack in this instance as the front hand of the square block is used to grab the sleeve and the rear or high hand of the block can either grab White's lapel or secure an underhook grip.

3. Black has completed the 270° turn and now has his hips firmly under White's thereby allowing him to completely disrupt White's balance to the point of lifting him off of the ground. It is important to use the broad, sweeping motion of the turn to load your opponent onto your hips, rather than trying to lift them with brute strength. Also note that Black is using the strength of his legs and hips to lift White off of the ground rather than trying to use the smaller muscles of the lower back.

4. Black continues the throwing technique by allowing White's momentum to continue over his back and onto the ground. It is important that Black keeps his feet under his hips in order to maintain stability.

5. After throwing White to the ground, it is important for Black to continue to control White to prevent any further attempts at a counterattack.

Step 1 *High Punch to Square Block*

Step 2 *High Punch to Square Block*

Step 3 *High Punch to Square Block*

Step 4 *High Punch to Square Block*

Step 5 *High Punch to Square Block*

High Block to Knifehand Strike

TECHNIQUE

Combination 4 – High Block to Knifehand Strike

APPLICATION

1. Black uses the high block technique as a simultaneous escape/elbow lock. When White grabs Black's wrist, Black must drop his body weight (front stance) to get his center of gravity below that of White. In doing so, it gives Black the leverage to pry White's grip off of his wrist while locking the elbow by applying upward pressure just above his elbow. While Black may not necessarily be able to break White's arm in this position, he is able to control White's balance leading to a counterattack.

2. Black sees that White is off balance and therefore removes the pressure from White's elbow. This allows Black to take advantage of White's disrupted balance to further his counterattack. Black uses the combination of the 270° turn and the chambering for the knifehand strike to pull White further off balance. Note that Black changes his hip position throughout the technique rather than trying to muscle White into the technique; this allows the technique

to be done smoothly and easily with great power, rather than jerky and fatiguing.

3. Black has completed the turn and has begun to execute the knifehand technique. Note that Black has grabbed White's wrist with his chambered hand and is using the knifehand against White's throat to better allow him to control White's movement.

4. Black will continue to pull with his right hand while striking with the left to move White off balance.

5. Black has completed the execution of the knifehand strike and has succeeded in taking White to the ground. By keeping the technique close to his body, Black is better able to utilize his hips in the takedown, thereby making it a more powerful technique. It is important to note that Black maintained control of White throughout the technique, including once he was on the ground.

Step 1 *High Block to Knifehand Strike*

Step 2 *High Block to Knifehand Strike*

Step 3 *High Block to Knifehand Strike*

Step 4 *High Block to Knifehand Strike*

Step 5 *High Block to Knifehand Strike*

Knifehand Strike to High Punch

TECHNIQUE

Combination 5 – Knifehand Strike to High Punch

APPLICATION

1. Black has attacked White by grabbing his right wrist and pulling it into himself while simultaneously striking White across the throat with a knifehand strike. Black was able to pull White off balance by using his hips to pull White's arm, rather than simply pulling with his arm. Black is also using his ribcage as a fulcrum to lock White's elbow. Black increases the pressure applied to White's elbow by pulling the wrist back to his hip and pushing backward with the arm in front of White's throat.

2. Once White has been taken off balance, Black continues the combination by sliding his hand from White's throat to his shoulder while using his other hand to grab White's wrist and moving into a wrist lock technique. Note that Black has positioned himself behind White so that he stays safely away from most of the weapons that White would use to counterattack.

3. Black has continued the previous movement by sliding his left hand from White's shoulder to his opposite arm. This prevents White from turning into Black and relieving the pressure on the shoulder lock. Black is combining the hip drive of the lunge punch with the stepping motion of the technique to further increase the pressure on White's shoulder.

Step 1 *Knifehand Strike to High Punch*

Step 2 *Knifehand Strike to High Punch*

Step 3 *Knifehand Strike to High Punch*

CHAPTER

6

Do-San

Do-San is the third pattern taught in the Taekwondo curriculum. Do-San was the pseudonym of the Korean patriot Ahn Chang-Ho. Ahn Chang-Ho is considered a patriot in Korean history for his role in the Korean Independence Movement from Japan. The Japanese maintained a crushing rule over the Korean people by disallowing the use of the Korean language, requiring the Korean people to adopt Japanese surnames, and closing Korean schools. Ahn Chang-Ho died in prison after being arrested for his work. The 24 movements of the pattern represent Ahn Chang-Ho's entire life, which was spent attempting to save Korean culture, history, education, and identity. The Do-San pattern represents a milestone for the Taekwondo student in that it introduces a series of firsts for the Taekwondo student. The first of these is the block and counterattack combination. Up until this point, the patterns would show a blocking technique following by a stepping attack. Do-San features a block followed by a striking technique while keeping the same stance. Do-San also incorporates the first instance of Taekwondo's trademark, which is of course, the kick. Lastly, Do-San incorporates the sitting stance, which gives the student the ability to sink his weight, which has many grappling applications.

Reverse Inner Forearm Block to Reverse Punch

TECHNIQUE

Combination 1 – Reverse Inner Forearm Block to Reverse Punch

APPLICATION

1. Black executes the reverse inner forearm block as a defense against White's cross-side wrist grab. By performing the circular motion of the block, Black is able to reverse White's grip and take control of White's attacking arm. Black also secures a grip on White's belt so that he can gain further control of White's movement via control over his hips. Note that Black's grip on White's belt could be modified to a position of the hand on the hip or grabbing the pants or shirt in that area.

2. Black finishes the technique by continuing to pull on White's arm while simultaneously pushing on White's hip. This push-pull action moves White's body along a spiral pathway making it difficult to maintain his balance. Because Black has kept his stance rather than stepping forward, he is now in a position to front kick White in his ribs or even round kick White's base leg out from under him.

Step 1 *Reverse Inner Forearm Block to Reverse Punch*

Step 2 *Reverse Inner Forearm Block to Reverse Punch*

Double Knifehand Block to Vertical Spearhand Strike

TECHNIQUE

Combination 2 – Double Knifehand Block to Vertical Spearhand Strike

APPLICATION

1. Black attacks White with a basic same-side lapel grab. By grasping both lapels at the same time, Black is also able to work toward a technique called the rope choke. Note that Black has also placed his left hand in a position over White's arm so that he has control over it. Black's right hand is positioned so that with a shift of the hips, he can push or pull White off balance.

2. Black keeps his grip on White's lapel and arm and proceeds to turn his hips away from White which results in White being pulled off balance. Note that it was Black's hip turn, not his arms, that pulled White toward him and off balance.

3. After gaining control over White's balance, Black has released the twin lapel grip with his right hand and replaced it with a cross lapel grab to White's opposite side. Simultaneously, Black has cupped his right hand across the other side of White's neck in order to control his position. With these hand positions, when Black attempts to move his arms into the double knifehand block position, the combination of the cupping action of the right arm and the pulling of the left arm will cause White to be pulled downward while looping the lapel under his neck.

4. Black continues the above motion and keeps his grip with his left hand deep inside White's lapel while extending his right hand over White's back into the spearhand position. In doing so, the downward spiraling motion of White is complete and the looping motion of the left hand pulls the lapel across White's throat while the spearhand simultaneously applies forward and downward pressure. The combination of Black's manipulations and White's movement results in a choke with the lapel across White's neck.

Step 1 *Double Knifehand Block to Vertical Spearhand Strike*

Step 2 *Double Knifehand Block to Vertical Spearhand Strike*

Step 3 *Double Knifehand Block to Vertical Spearhand Strike*

Step 4 *Double Knifehand Block to Vertical Spearhand Strike (with alternate view)*

Vertical Spearhand Strike to High Backfist Strike

TECHNIQUE

Combination 3 – Vertical Spearhand Strike to High Backfist Strike

APPLICATION

1. White attacks Black with a basic same-side wrist grab. White's attack is noteworthy in that it allows White the opportunity to control Black's balance as well as giving him a handle that he can use to control Black's movements. Additionally, White is also in a position to strike Black with his right hand while not giving Black an avenue of escape. Black uses the motion of the spearhand strike combined with a twisting of the wrist to move his hand to a thumb down position to break/loosen White's grip on it.

2. Seeing the striking attack from White, Black uses the spinning transition from the spearhand to the backfist strike to evade the punching attack, complete the escape from the wrist grab, obtain a grip on White's sleeve, and

gain an underhook. Black uses the momentum of the turn to pull White off balance and into his body, rather than attempting to pull him into the technique.

3. Black continues the turning motion of the combination while simultaneously lifting up on White's left arm with his underhook and pulling on his right arm with his left hand. Notice that throughout the combination; Black's weight continues to drop, placing him below White's hips, giving him the leverage to complete the throw. It is important to notice in this combination that it is the principle of the combination that causes the grappling application to occur, rather than the specific techniques.

Step 1 *Vertical Spearhand Strike to High Backfist Strike*

Step 2 *Vertical Spearhand Strike to High Backfist Strike*

Step 3 *Vertical Spearhand Strike to High Backfist Strike*

Twin Reverse Inner Forearm Block to Front Kick

TECHNIQUE

Combination 1 – Twin Reverse Inner Forearm Block to Front Kick

APPLICATION

1. In an example of a common grappling exchange, White has attacked Black with a twin lapel grab and Black has responded with a twin lapel grab of his own. Once locked in this position, inexperienced grapplers tend to engage in nothing more than a shoving match with generally no one getting the advantage through anything but luck.

2. Black uses the twin reverse inner forearm block to spread White's arms apart. Spreading White's arms will give Black the space he needs to begin a takedown technique. Black drives his foot deep into White's midsection in a thrusting motion. While this thrusting motion may have the effect of a kick on White, it is more important that Black push White's hips backward to off balance him. Black

uses his grip combined with his foot in White's midsection to execute the takedown. Note that Black does not pull White into him to the ground; rather Black simply removes his base leg from the ground and sits down. This allows Black to use the dead weight of his body to pull White to the ground.

3. Black continues his backward momentum while maintaining his grip on White's lapels and keeping his foot in White's midsection. As White nears the ground behind Black's head, Black will begin to initiate a backward roll of his own so that he finishes the technique sitting atop White in the mount position.

Step 1 *Twin Reverse Inner Forearm Block to Front Kick*

Step 2 *Twin Reverse Inner Forearm Block to Front Kick*

Step 3 *Twin Reverse Inner Forearm Block to Front Kick*

Twin Reverse Inner Forearm Block to Front Kick to Lunge Punch to Reverse Punch

TECHNIQUE

Combination 5 – Twin Reverse Inner Forearm Block to Front Kick to Lunge Punch to Reverse Punch

APPLICATION

1. The initial position for this application begins much like that of the previous application. It is important for strikers to spend time in this position as it is a position in which grapplers are quite comfortable.

2. Instead of placing the front kick in White's midsection, Black front kicks past White's leg and uses the re-chambering portion of the kick to hook behind White's leg. Note that as Black extends the kick past White, he pushes White's shoulders back to begin to take him off balance.

3. The off-balancing is complete as Black continues to push White's shoulders while driving the hooking leg further into White.

4. Black uses the punching techniques of the combination as control and finishing techniques. Black uses the left lunge punch to force White's back down to the ground thereby giving Black more control over his movement.

5. In this example, the right reverse punch is used a choke as Black grabs the lapel with his right hand and drives it to the ground across White's throat. By controlling White in this way, Black has many options whereas White can only attempt to turn away from Black to escape the choke, which would be a course of action that would give Black an unimpeded opportunity to strike with his left hand or simply escape.

Step 1 *Twin Reverse Inner Forearm Block to Front Kick to Lunge Punch to Reverse Punch*

Step 2 & 3 *Twin Reverse Inner Forearm Block to Front Kick to Lunge Punch to Reverse Punch*

Step 4 & 5 *Twin Reverse Inner Forearm Block to Front Kick to Lunge Punch to Reverse Punch*

Won-Hyo

The fourth pattern in the Taekwondo curriculum, Won-Hyo which was the religious name of the monk responsible for introducing Buddhism to the Silla Dynasty of Korea in 686 A.D. Won-Hyo was the pen name of Sol-Sedang, a prolific writer with over 240 volumes spanning 100 different types of literature to his credit. The name Won-Hyo, which means "Breaking Dawn" refers to his role in establishing Buddhism in Korean culture, or the "first dawning" of Buddhism on earth. Won-Hyo is considered to be one of the leading writers, thinkers, and commentators of Korean Buddhism of his time. Won-Hyo's success in disseminating Buddhism across Korea comes from the fact that he was able to extend its reach beyond the Royal family to the common people. This was a most difficult task as many of the scrolls central to Buddhism were only written in Chinese, a language not understood by the common person. The Won-Hyo pattern introduces many firsts to the practitioner; among these is the first use of the style's trademark side kick. Other firsts introduced are the multiple hand technique combination, as well as attacking and defending against attacks from multiple directions.

Square Block to Inward Knifehand Strike

TECHNIQUE

Combination 1 – Square Block to Inward Knifehand Strike

APPLICATION

1. White attacks Black with a twin wrist grab. This is a common attack faced by many outside the walls of the dojang. With this attack, White can easily pull Black off balance or even throw him to the ground. From this position, it is difficult for Black to maintain his balance and avoid moving in any direction other than the one White desires.

2. Black uses the circular motion of the hips and arms during the execution of the square block to pull White off balance and into him. Note that by emphasizing the block's circular nature Black frees himself from White's grip on his left hand and White is now overextended in trying to maintain his grip on Black's right hand. White is now vulnerable to a counterattack by Black as Black is stable and in a position to strike.

3. Black pulls his free left hand to his hips and uses the circular action of his hips to drive a knifehand strike with his right hand into White's throat. Note the change in the position of Black's hips from the previous picture to this one. By turning his hips into his knifehand strike and pulling White's hand to his hip, Black simultaneously keeps White off balance while delivering a powerful strike to his attacker. Also note the position of Black's lead foot. He is in a position to perform a front leg sweep to White's leg while striking him to ensure that White is taken off balance and to the ground.

Step 1 *Square Block to Inward Knifehand Strike*

Step 2 *Square Block to Inward Knifehand Strike*

Step 3 *Square Block to Inward Knifehand Strike*

Square Block to Inward Knifehand Strike to Lunge Punch

TECHNIQUE

Combination 2 – Square Block to Inward Knifehand Strike to Lunge Punch

APPLICATION

1. White attacks Black with the same twin wrist grab from the previous combination only this time he does so from behind. Black defends by using the circular motion of the square block in much the same way.

2. However, because of the nature of White's attack, Black simultaneously turns his body into the technique. This turn allows Black to create space between him and White thereby giving him more options to counterattack. Also note that by shifting his weight to his rear leg, Black gives himself the ability to strike with his front leg.

3. Black utilizes the knifehand strike/lunge punch combination in a different way to show the versatility of the combination. By using the lead hand for the knifehand strike, Black completely disrupts White's balance by combining the knifehand strike with a powerful hip movement in the same direction.

4. Black shifts his hips back in the other direction to utilize the punching technique as a takedown by continuing to push White in the direction in which he is falling.

Step 1 & 2 *Square Block to Inward Knifehand Strike to Lunge Punch*

Step 3 & 4 *Square Block to Inward Knifehand Strike to Lunge Punch*

Double Knifehand Block to Double Knifehand Block

TECHNIQUE

Combination 3 – Double Knifehand Block to Double Knifehand Block

APPLICATION

1. White attacks Black from behind with a twin rear shoulder grab. From this position, it would be very easy for White to pull Black backward and down to the ground.

2. Black begins the defense by turning into White and using the chambering technique for the double knifehand block to split White's grip and gain control over one of White's wrists and the back of his head.

3. Black continues the forward motion of the double knifehand block by increasing the torque on White's wrist and pulling his head with the other hand. It is important to note that Black's hips are powering his control over White's movement, not simply his arms and shoulders. By simultaneously pulling on the head while locking the wrist, Black has effectively broken White's balance as evidenced by White's weight being pushed forward onto his front foot.

4. Black guides White around his body and attacks White's neck with his opposite arm.

5. From this position, Black begins to execute the second double knifehand block. Note that the second double knifehand block is not as visible, but it is there when the movement is performed. By securing a grip on White's jaw and lapel, Black begins the chambering phase of the block. By attempting to perform the block fully, Black's grip on White's lapel results in the collar being pulled across his neck in a choking technique. White's movement is controlled because of the neck lock Black has secured on him. If a neck lock is not desired, Black simply needs to turn White's body so that his head faces the ground and the result will be a guillotine choke.

Step 1 & 2 *Double Knifehand Block to Double Knifehand Block*

Step 3 *Double Knifehand Block to Double Knifehand Block*

Step 4 & 5 *Double Knifehand Block to Double Knifehand Block*

Spearhand Strike to Square Block

TECHNIQUE

Combination 4 – Spearhand Strike to Square Block

APPLICATION

1. White attacks Black with a basic lapel grab that allows him some degree of control over Black's movement. White would typically combine this type of grab with a quick shove followed by a punching technique when Black is off balance.

2. Black quickly counters White's grab however by using the spearhand technique to trap White's arm to his chest and "spear" the right arm under White's armpit to secure an underhook.

3. Black utilizes the 270° turn between the spearhand strike and the square block to further secure his underhook.

4. Black uses the momentum of the turn to load White onto and over his hips. Note the turning of Black's hips throughout the combination is the impetus for the technique, rather than simple brute strength.

5. By finishing with the square block, Black maintains firm control over White once he is on the ground.

Step 1 & 2 *Spearhand Strike to Square Block*

Step 3, 4 & 5
*Spearhand Strike to
Square Block*

Reverse Punch to Scooping Block

TECHNIQUE

Combination 5 – Reverse Punch to Scooping Block

APPLICATION

1. White attacks Black with a cross-side wrist grab. This attack can give White a slight advantage over Black as it gives him the opportunity to pull Black into striking attacks that he may attempt to deliver.

2. Black counters this grab by using the initial hip shift for the reverse punch to pull White into him and slightly off balance.

3. Black then uses the force of the reverse punch to disrupt White's grip on his arm, thereby freeing him from White's grasp.

4. Immediately after executing the reverse punch, Black uses his other hand to secure his own grip on White's wrist. This allows Black to set-up his counterattack with the scooping block.

5. Black drops his weight into a front stance and executes the scooping block under and around White's arm. The hip action utilized during the block allows him to lock White's shoulder and force him to bend forward at the waist. From this position, Black has the opportunity to escape or counterattack with strikes or kicks.

Step 1, 2 & 3
Reverse Punch to Scooping Block

Step 4 & 5 *Reverse Punch to Scooping Block*

CHAPTER 8

Yul-Gok

The fifth pattern in the Taekwondo curriculum is named for Yul-Gok, which was the pseudonym of the philosopher Yi I, commonly known as "The Confucius of Korea." Yul-Gok was much like Won-Hyo in that he was considered a prodigy from birth. He was able to read Chinese script at the age of three and by the time he was seven, he was composing poetry in Chinese, and had finished his schooling in Confucianism and the Classics. Six short years later, at the age of 13, he had passed the civil service exam for the literary department. During his adult life, he authored many books on Confucian life and after he died, "The Complete Works of Yul-Gok" was published. In addition to his literary accolades, Yul-Gok was also active in governmental issues, specifically in the area of reform. The Yul-Gok pattern is the longest to date for the Taekwondo practitioner at a lengthy 38 movements. A few movements that are new to the Taekwondo practitioner are among them. These include the hooking block, which has many grappling applications, as well as the elbow strike, which in addition to being a powerful striking weapon, has grappling applications as well.

Sitting Stance Punch to Sitting Stance Punch to Outer Forearm Block

TECHNIQUE

Combination 1 – Sitting Stance Punch to Sitting Stance Punch to Outer Forearm Block

APPLICATION

1. Black uses the first punch in the combination as a grabbing attack to White's shoulder.

2. In doing so, it allows him to use the push/pull motion of the second punching attack to pull White forward and off balance while grabbing White's other wrist.

3. Finally, Black uses the wrist grab to push White's elbow upward giving him the space to apply the outer forearm block to White's shoulder, effectively executing a standing shoulder lock.

Step 1 & 2
*Sitting Stance Punch to Sitting Stance
Punch to Outer Forearm Block*

Step 3
*Sitting Stance Punch to Sitting Stance
Punch to Outer Forearm Block*

Hooking Block to Hooking Block to Reverse Punch

TECHNIQUE

Combination 2 – Hooking Block to Hooking Block to Reverse Punch

APPLICATION

1. White attacks Black with a basic lapel grab that would allow him to gain control over Black's movement. With this attack, White has the ability to push Black backward into a wall or some other obstruction as well as having the ability to pull him into a strike with his other hand. Black immediately begins to counterattack White by turning his body into White's grab which results in White's shoulder and elbow being locked.

2. Black then turns his hips the other direction and executes the first hooking block to the outside of White's arm thereby gaining control over his arm.

3. Black continues the counterattack by executing the second hooking block which gives him control over White's arm and utilizes the reverse punch as a grabbing attack to White's chest/shoulder/throat.

4. Black then adds a basic stepping technique to the combination, resulting in White being forcefully taken to the ground through a basic push/pull motion inherent in punching attacks.

Step 1 & 2 *Hooking Block to Hooking Block to Reverse Punch*

Step 3 & 4 *Hooking Block to Hooking Block to Reverse Punch*

Guarding Block to Side Kick to Inward Elbow Strike

TECHNIQUE

Combination 3 – Guarding Block to Side Kick to Inward Elbow Strike

APPLICATION

1. Black attacks White from the side and secures a lapel grab. A lapel grab from this angle would allow Black to maneuver White into various takedown and throwing techniques.

2. As Black snaps his hips to the side, he releases his grip on the lapel and turns it into a partial choke around White's neck. At the same time, Black executes a side kick to the back of White's knee, which drops his body weight toward the ground, thereby increasing the pressure applied from the arm around his throat.

3. After the side kick which resulted in White on his knees and Black behind him, Black finds himself in a position to finish the combination by locking in the choking technique. Note the position of the hands after the execution of an inward elbow strike. Recall that when executing an elbow strike in a pattern, the strike is typically done into an open palm resulting in a squared position of the arms. Utilize this same position and use the striking arm to apply pressure to the back of the neck. This pressure, when combined with the pressure from the arm in front of the neck results in a powerful choking technique.

Step 1 & 2
*Guarding Block to Side Kick to
Inward Elbow Strike*

Step 3
*Guarding Block to Side Kick to
Inward Elbow Strike*

Inward Elbow Strike to Square Block

TECHNIQUE

Combination 4 – Inward Elbow Strike to Square Block

APPLICATION

1. Black is using the inward elbow strike from the previous combination as a rear naked choke. Be sure the arm in front is snugly under the chin and the arm in the back is locked securely onto the biceps of the front arm.

2. With the choke firmly secured, Black begins the 180° turn into the square and pushes his hips into the back of White's, thereby off-balancing him backward and onto Black's hips.

3. Black continues the throwing motion by lifting with his hips while keeping the choke secure. The result is White being pulled over Black's back.

4. This is a particularly brutal throw as White lands face down rather than on his back. Once White hits the ground, Black continues to apply pressure to the choke until he can escape or White submits.

Step 1 & 2 *Inward Elbow Strike to Square Block*

Step 3 & 4 *Inward Elbow Strike to Square Block*

Square Block to Spearhand Strike to Square Block

TECHNIQUE

Combination 5 – Square Block to Spearhand Strike to Square Block

APPLICATION

1. Black attacks White with a twin wrist grab which allows him a good deal of control over White's movement.

2. Black uses the control gained from the wrist grab to move into the square block and pull White forward and off balance. Note that Black's hips are powering the movement, not just his arms.

3. Black takes advantage of White's temporary loss of balance to slip the spearhand strike underneath White's armpit thereby securing an underhook on him and eliminating his ability to use his arms to counterattack.

4. Black then uses the turning motion before the next square block to pivot his hips and tighten his underhook. This allows Black to begin to load White onto his hip and continue the combination.

5. As Black completes the 180° turn, he has completely loaded White onto his hip and is using the combination of upward leg drive, hip lift, and pulling with the underhook to throw White over his body.

6. The combination is completed when Black uses a variation of the final hand position of the square block to secure White's arm and control his movement on the ground.

Step 1 & 2
*Square Block to Spearhand
Strike to Square Block*

Step 3 & 4
*Square Block to Spearhand
Strike to Square Block*

Step 5 & 6 *Square Block to Spearhand Strike to Square Block*

CHAPTER

9

Joong-Gun

The sixth pattern in the Taekwondo curriculum is named after An Joong-Gun, a Korean patriot and well-known educator in late 19th, early 20th century Korea. Like many other educators of that time, An Joong-Gun's school, the Sam-Heung (Three Success) School, was hard hit by the Japanese occupation of Korea. The Japanese occupation was especially harsh with the Japanese applying great pressure on the Korean government to sign a treaty accepting the occupation and Japanese statesman Hirobumi Ito as the Japanese resident general of Korea in 1905. As a result of the oppression by the Japanese, An Joong-Gun left Korea for southern Manchuria. It was during this time that he formed a small army and conducted raids across the border into Korea resulting in a constant harassment of the Japanese oppressors. The Japanese attempted to brutally squelch the rebellion by the Korean guerillas and as a result, there were many deaths on both sides due to both combat actions and assassinations. Eventually, the Japanese attempted to sell native Korean lands, which ultimately resulted in An-Joong Gun's martyrdom. Upon hearing news of the attempted land sale, An Joong-Gun began to plan for the assassination of Hirobumi Ito. On October 26, 1909, An Joong-Gun put his plan into action and successfully assassinated Hirobumi Ito as he stepped off of a train. As a result, he was tortured for months until he was executed in March of 1910. The 32 movements in the pattern represent the years of An Joong-Gun's life. The Joong-Gun pattern introduces many new techniques to the practitioner, such as the ridgehand block, twin striking techniques such as the twin high and upset punches and the upward X and U shaped blocks. These techniques have a great deal of grappling applications which can be seen on the following pages.

Upward Elbow Strike to Double Knifehand Block

TECHNIQUE

Combination 1 – Upward Elbow Strike to Double Knifehand Block

APPLICATION

1. After having been attacked with a basic grabbing attack by White, Black moves to the outside of White's arm and applies the upward elbow strike to the underside of White's arm. By pulling down on White's wrist while applying upward pressure to his elbow, Black is locking White's elbow and controlling his movement.

2. With White taken off balance by the elbow locking technique, Black releases the pressure and executes a double knifehand block. By executing the block over the locked arm, the forward hand acts as a strike to the chest/throat of White. The combination of the striking motion of the lead arm and the pulling motion with the rear arm results in White being thrown backward. Note that Black can also alter his stance so that his lead foot is behind White's, resulting in a full takedown technique.

Step 1 *Upward Elbow Strike to Double Knifehand Block*

Step 2 *Upward Elbow Strike to Double Knifehand Block*

Guarding Block to Twin Pressing Palm

TECHNIQUE

Combination 2 – Guarding Block to Twin Pressing Palm

APPLICATION

1. As White attacks Black with a same-side shoulder grab with which he could swing Black off balance, Black counterattacks by using the guarding block as a same-side shoulder grab of his own. By grabbing White, Black is able to use White's body mass as a counterbalance in the event that White attempts to move him off balance.

2. Black uses the twin pressing palm as an elbow lock for his counterattack. Black accomplishes this by sliding his shoulder grip down to the wrist while applying upward pressure to the underside of White's arm with the rising hand of the pressing palm. The simultaneous downward pressure at the wrist and upward pressure just above the elbow result in an elbow lock on White. With this pressure, Black is able to keep White off balance long enough to escape or to counter with a strike.

Step 1 *Guarding Block to Twin Pressing Palm*

Step 2 *Guarding Block to Twin Pressing Palm*

Twin Pressing Palm to Hook Punch

TECHNIQUE

Combination 3 – Twin Pressing Palm to Hook Punch

APPLICATION

1. Black uses the pressing palm in much the same way as before, to lock the elbow joint and control White's movement. This time however, Black uses the twin pressing palm as an attacking technique to lead into further attacks. It is important to note, that while this may not be the most painful of the joint-locking techniques, when performed correctly, it gives the user a good sense of control over their opponent.

2. After taking White off balance, Black releases the elbow lock and moves into the hook punch. By pulling White's wrist, Black continues to keep White not only off balance, but moving in a direction that Black wants.

3. As Black completes the execution of the hook punch, combined with the pulling of White's wrist, White's balance is completely disrupted and he can be easily taken to the ground.

Step 1
*Twin Pressing Palm
to Hook Punch*

Step 2 & 3
*Twin Pressing Palm
to Hook Punch*

Hook Punch to C-Block

TECHNIQUE

Combination 4 – Hook Punch to C-Block

APPLICATION

1. Black uses the hook punch's circular motion as a trap for the roundhouse kick executed by White. Note that Black's lead hand is still in a position to defend against follow-up attacks by White and his feet are in a balanced position to help him absorb the force of White's kick.

2. Black completes the hooking motion of the punch and in doing so, forces White's knee to point toward the ground. This manipulation of White's leg makes him easy to control and puts his balance entirely in Black's hands.

3. Black then executes the C-Block explosively with a slightly upward trajectory which pushes White's leg back toward his body and completely off balance.

Step 1 *Hook Punch to C-Block*

Step 2 *Hook Punch to C-Block*

Step 3 *Hook Punch to C-Block*

C-Block to C-Block

TECHNIQUE

Combination 5 – C-Block to C-Block

APPLICATION

1. Black uses the first C-Block as the entry into a take-down technique. Black uses the top hand to pull downward on White's collar or the back of his neck to off-balance him.

2. Black's lower hand is used to move between White's legs and lift him upward to set up the takedown. Note that Black's position is stable and he is in a position to move quickly and powerfully.

3. Black's simultaneous pulling of the neck and lifting at the hips has resulted in White being pull off balance and onto his back. Note that Black's position allows him to absorb White's weight so that he is not having to physically "lift and hold" White for an extended period of time.

4. By being stable with his hips, Black can allow his shoulders to dip once White is loaded, thereby controlling where he is thrown.

Step 1 & 2 *C-Block to C-Block*

Step 3 & 4 *C-Block to C-Block*

CHAPTER 10

Toi-Gye

Toi-Gye is the seventh pattern in the Taekwondo curriculum. Toi-Gye, which means "returning stream," is the pen name of Yi Hwang, a 16th century scholar best known for his writings that are seen as a major influence on neo-Confucianism. The foundation of his school of thought is the proposition that "li" (reason) and "chi" (vital force) were responsible for all human characteristics. His viewpoint was very similar to the idea of the body and soul in Western thought. Toi-Gye's scholarly influence led him into the political world where he focused on political and religious reform. The Toi-Gye pattern introduces many techniques such as the mountain block, the fingertip strike, and the knee kick.

Mountain Block to Downward Block

TECHNIQUE

Combination 1 – Mountain Block to Downward Block

APPLICATION

1. White attacks Black with a cross-side shoulder grab. While seemingly innocuous, this grab will allow White to turn Black's shoulder giving him access to his back.

2. Black counters the grabbing with the mountain block. Black counterattacks by grabbing White's attacking hand and moving to the side off of the line of attack. As Black moves to the side, he uses the other hand to strike the back of White's arm just above the elbow. The simultaneous push/pull at the wrist and elbow results in an elbow lock.

3. Black continues the combination by keeping his grip on White's attacking hand and sliding his other arm that was at White's elbow over White's arm and executes a downward block. Note the change in the position of Black's hips throughout the combination. By turning his hips, Black has the power to break down White's arm and pull him off balance. Also note how Black constantly manipulates White's balance throughout the combination by first off-balancing him forward and then backward. This constant changing of position does not give White a chance to stabilize himself enough to attempt a counterattack.

Step 1 & 2
Mountain Block to Downward Block

Step 3
*Mountain Block to
Downward Block*

Twin Neck Grab to Upward Knee Kick

TECHNIQUE

Combination 2 – Twin Neck Grab to Upward Knee Kick

APPLICATION

Black utilizes this combination as a controlling technique to be used once he has taken White to the ground. Black uses the twin neck grab around the back of White's neck while simultaneously driving his knee into White's sternum. This combination of movements results in two techniques, each of which could be used to control White. The first, as a result of the twin neck grab is what is known in grappling as a neck crank. The second technique with the knee on the chest results in a type of choke that works by not allowing the chest to expand to allow air into the lungs. The combination of both makes for a devastating combination.

Twin Neck Grab to Upward Knee Kick

Backfist/Downward Block to Jumping Low 'X' Block

TECHNIQUE

Combination 3 – Backfist/Downward Block to Jumping Low 'X' Block

APPLICATION

1. Black uses the backfist/downward block combination as a defense against a twin lapel grab by White. Black uses the circular nature combined with the powerful hip action of the technique to free himself from White's grasp while pulling White off balance thereby setting him up for further attacks.

2. After stepping backward during the backfist/downward block defense resulting in White being pulled off balance in the forward direction, Black immediately moves forward for the jumping low 'X' block to push White off balance in the backward direction. Note that Black keeps control over White's arms and keeps his body to the outside of White's, protecting him from counterattacks. Note the position of Black's lead leg. It is applying pressure to the outside of White's knee while the lead foot is hooked behind White's lead foot.

3. Black finishes the combination by continuing his forward motion. Black has taken White to the ground because his forward momentum applied pressure to White's knee while Black's lead foot prevented White from stepping backward. The result is White's knee slamming into the ground allowing Black to escape or continue with strikes.

Step 1
*Backfist/Downward
Block to Jumping
Low 'X' Block*

Step 2 *Backfist/Downward Block to Jumping 'X' Block*

Step 3
*Backfist/Downward Block to
Jumping Low 'X' Block*

Low Double Knifehand Block to Circular Block

TECHNIQUE

Combination 4 – Low Double Knifehand Block to Circular Block

APPLICATION

1. White attacks Black with a same-side lapel grab. This type of grabbing attack gives White some semblance of control over Black's movement, but more importantly, it prevents Black from moving away from White if White begins to attack with strikes.

2. Black counterattacks by performing a low double knifehand block. The low double knifehand block allows Black to weaken White's grip on his lapel while taking him off balance. Black uses his other hand to pull White's other arm into him which results in a greater ability for Black to defend against any strikes White may attempt.

3. With his grip on White's left arm, Black executes the circular block underneath White's right arm. This completely negates any ability White has to strike and it puts Black in control of the situation. From this position, Black could easily finish the confrontation with knee strikes to White's exposed ribcage or a sweep to White's weighted leg.

Step 1 & 2
*Low Double Knifehand
Block to Circular Block*

Step 3
*Low Double Knifehand
Block to Circular Block*

Circular Block to Circular Block

TECHNIQUE

Combination 5 – Circular Block to Circular Block

APPLICATION

1. White attacks Black with a same-side lapel grab. This type of grabbing attack gives White some semblance of control over Black's movement, but more importantly, it prevents Black from moving away if White begins to attack with strikes.

2. In this combination, Black uses the first circular block as a way to drop his weight onto White's attacking limb, rather than as a block or strike. Black drops the circular block against White's attacking arm with his body weight to break White's balance forward and bend the arm.

3. Black uses the second circular block around White's neck as a variation of the guillotine choking technique known as the "Willotine." By keeping his weight on the back of White's neck while lifting with the choking arm, Black is applying a great amount of pressure to White's throat.

Step 1 & 2 *Circular Block to Circular Block*

Step 3 *Circular Block to Circular Block (with alternate view)*

CHAPTER

11

Hwa-Rang

The eighth pattern in the Taekwondo curriculum, Hwa-Rang, is unique in that rather than being named for a specific person, it was named for a group of people, the Hwa-Rang youth group of the 6th century Silla Dynasty. The Hwa-Rang, which is translated as "Flower of Knighthood", were young men of nobility chosen for their handsomeness and virtue. These groups consisted of thousands of members and their leaders, called Kuk-Son, often became government officials, military leaders, and even kings of the Silla Dynasty. The Hwa-Rang were educated in many traditional academic areas such as literature, dance, and science, but they were also trained extensively in archery and hand-to-hand combat. The Hwa-Rang, often compared to the Samurai of Japan, had a code for which they are well known: loyalty to king and country, obedience to one's parents, sincerity among friends, never retreating in battle, and justice in killing. In fact, the nine virtues of the Hwa-Rang, humanity, justice, courtesy, wisdom, trust, goodness, virtue, loyalty, and courage, are found in the current tenets of Taekwondo. Hwa-Rang introduces new techniques to the Taekwondo practitioner such as the sitting stance palm strike, high roundhouse kicks, and use of the vertical stance.

Square Block to Upset Punch to Lunge Punch

TECHNIQUE

Combination 1 – Square Block to Upset Punch to Lunge Punch

APPLICATION

1. Black attacks White with a twin wrist grab.

2. Rather than trying to pull White off balance, Black immediately twists his hips and executes a square block which results in White being turned and pulled forward. This results in Black being in a position to avoid counterattacks from White as well as giving Black access to White's back.

3. Black uses his access to White's back as a result of the square block to use the upset punch as a choking technique. Note that Black's arm is snugly under White's chin and his elbow is pointing down toward his hips in line with White's sternum.

4. Black locks in or "sinks" the choke by executing the lunge punch over White's shoulder. Black then secures his grip on the choke by grabbing the biceps of the lunge punch arm with the upset punch arm.

Step 1 & 2 *Square Block to Upset Punch to Lunge Punch*

Step 3 & 4 *Square Block to Upset Punch to Lunge Punch*

Lunge Punch to Downward Knifehand Strike

TECHNIQUE

Combination 2 – Lunge Punch to Downward Knifehand Strike

APPLICATION

1. White attacks Black with a same-side lapel grab. With this attack, White is able to pull Black into follow-up punching attacks in addition to turning Black so that White can gain access to his back. Black counters this grab by executing the lunge punch under White's attacking arm. While punching his arm underneath White's attacking arm, Black also drives his shoulder into White's upper arm while pulling on White's sleeve. The combination of these actions pulls White off balance.

2. Black takes advantage of White's temporary loss of balance to begin the execution of the downward knifehand strike. Black utilizes the low position he assumed during the lunge punch to use his legs to drive him upward during the initial phase of the knifehand strike.

3. While keeping his grip on White's sleeve, Black takes advantage of the inherent structure of the elbow and shoulder and sweeps his arm along the downward arc of the circle. This results in White's shoulder being locked while Black is able to execute a painful shoulder or hammer lock on White's arm.

Step 1
*Lunge Punch to Down-
ward Knifehand Strike*

Step 2 & 3
*Lunge Punch to Downward
Knifehand Strike*

Downward Knifehand Strike to Lunge Punch to Downward Block

TECHNIQUE

Combination 3 – Downward Knifehand Strike to Lunge Punch to Downward Block

APPLICATION

1. White attacks Black with a cross-side wrist grab.

2. Black counterattacks by using the initial phase of the circular motion of the downward knifehand to pull his arm away from White's grasp.

3. Black completes the circle on the downward knifehand strike and gains control over White's attacking arm.

4. Black keeps control over White's attacking wrist and uses the lunge punch across White's throat. The combination of the Black's pulling with his right hand on White's wrist with the back pressure on White's throat from the lunge punch results in White being off balance.

5. With White off balance from Black's earlier combination of attacks, it is easy for Black to completely disrupt White's balance. Black swings the leg on the blocking side backward in a circle so that he can use the power of his hips to execute the downward block.

6. Black then executes the downward block while holding onto White's wrist resulting in White being taken backward to the ground where Black maintains control over him.

Step 1, 2 & 3 *Downward Knifehand Strike to Lunge Punch to Downward Block*

Step 4
*Downward Knifehand
Strike to Lunge Punch
to Downward Block*

Step 5 & 6 *Downward Knifehand Strike to Lunge Punch to Downward Block*

Pull to Side Kick

TECHNIQUE

Combination 4 – Pull to Side Kick

APPLICATION

1. Black attacks White from behind, using the fist in palm technique as a rear naked choke. By keeping his elbow in line with White's sternum and pulling back toward his body, Black applies pressure to White's carotid arteries.

2. Black then executes the side kick to the back of White's knee, collapsing his base and creating a "hanging" effect that increases the pressure on the choke.

Step 1 *Pull to Side Kick*

Step 2 *Pull to Side Kick*

Round Kick to Double Knifehand Block to Downward Block

TECHNIQUE

Combination 5 – Round Kick to Double Knifehand Block to Downward Block

APPLICATION

1. White attacks Black with a same-side lapel grab. While not the most dangerous grabbing attack, it does give White the advantage in that it gives him the ability to push or pull Black quite easily.

2. Black counters the grab by using the round kick to the ankle region of the leg as a foot sweep. While this won't take White completely off of his feet, it will momentarily disrupt his balance giving Black an opportunity to continue his counterattack.

3. With White off balance, Black uses the double knife-hand block as a means to further off-balance White.

4. Black then grabs White's lapel as he begins the down-ward block.

5. Black then snaps his hips and executes the downward block, pulling the off-balance White to the ground.

Step 1 & 2 *Round Kick to Double Knifehand Block to Downward Block*

Step 3, 4 & 5 *Round Kick to Double Knifehand Block to Downward Block*

Choong-Moo

Choong-Moo is the ninth pattern in the Taekwondo curriculum and in many organizations the last color-belt pattern. Choong-Moo is the actual name of Yi Sun-Sin, a 16th century admiral who was responsible for naval operations during the Choson Dynasty and defeated the Japanese in both 1592 and 1598. Choong-Moo is also famous for being the inventor of the Kobukson, a ship with iron plates over four inch thick wood to protect soldiers and rowers on the ship. The ship was said to resemble a turtle and even had a turtle-shaped battering ram on its front. Sailors on the ship were able to fire smoke, arrows, and missiles from the mouth of the turtle. In addition to this opening in the front, the Kobukson had another similar opening in the back as well as six more on both sides of the ship. Lastly, the iron shell had spikes and knives attached to it to thwart ramming by other ships. As if this weaponry and armor were not enough, the Kobukson was also heavier and faster than anything on the water at that time. The excellent construction of the Kobukson combined with Choong-Moo's gift for naval tactics made for a nearly unbeatable combination. Choong-Moo is considered to be one of the greatest heroes in Korean history. The pattern is unique in that it ends with a left hand attack. The left hand symbolizes Admiral Yi's unfortunate death and in Buddhist tradition, the left hand symbolizes a state of enlightenment. Choong-Moo introduces new kicking techniques to the Taekwondo practitioner such as the flying side kick and spinning back kick.

Knifehand Square Block to High Block/Inward Knifehand Strike

TECHNIQUE

Combination 1 – Knifehand Square Block to High Block/Inward Knifehand Strike

APPLICATION

1. White attacks Black with a twin wrist grab. This attack gives White complete control over Black's arms and allows him to pull Black in any direction he chooses. Black counters the grab by executing the square block as a parrying technique to throw White off balance while bringing his arms closer to his body while simultaneously pulling White's away from his. It is important to note that the position of the arms relative to the body has a great effect on how much force the arms can produce.

2. Black uses the high block to lift White's arm up and backward while using the inward knifehand to force the elbow to bend. From that position, Black is able to gain complete control over White's arm. With White's arm locked in Black's as it is in step 2, Black can use that bent arm as leverage to take White to the ground.

Step 1 *Knifehand Square Block to High Block/Inward Knifehand Strike*

Step 2 *Knifehand Square Block to High Block/Inward Knifehand Strike*

Twin Neck Grab to Knee Kick to Ridgehand Strike

TECHNIQUE

Combination 2 – Twin Neck Grab to Knee Kick to Ridgehand Strike

APPLICATION

1. Black uses the twin neck grab as a plum grip to gain control over White's movement by controlling the position of his head. From this position, by turning his hips, Black can pull White wherever he wants him to go.

2. Black uses the knee kick as a thrusting movement to get in close to perform a throw on White. Alternatively, Black can drive his knee into White's thigh to soften him up for the impending throw.

3. Black slides one arm from the plum position of his arms around the back of White's neck and uses that grip as leverage, combined with the thrusting motion of the knee kick to load White onto his back.

4. Black then continues to pull on White's head while lifting with his hips to pull White over his hips and onto the ground in front of him.

Step 1 & 2
Twin Neck Grab to Knee Kick to Ridgehand Strike

Step 3 & 4 *Twin Neck Grab to Knee Kick to Ridgehand Strike*

Rear Backfist/Downward Block to Spearhand Strike

TECHNIQUE

Combination 3 – Rear Backfist/Downward Block to Spearhand Strike

APPLICATION

1. White attacks Black with a same-side wrist grab. While this attack seems as though it would not have much of an effect on Black, White can use it to immobilize Black briefly so that he can attempt to strike him.

2. White uses his grabbing attack to immobilize Black so that he can front kick him to his midsection. In fact, Black's natural reaction to back up will allow White's kick to reach full extension before it makes contact, thereby making it more powerful.

3. Black uses the circular nature of the downward block portion of the combination to parry White's leg and catch it. Black does this while simultaneously pulling his other hand into the backfist position. By doing these movements in tandem, Black now has control over White's leg and arm.

This makes it very difficult for White to do anything except try to maintain his balance.

4. Black uses the forward motion of the spearhand strike to step into White completing the disruption of his balance. Black releases his grip on White's wrist and executes the spearhand strike under White's arm as a grab around White's waist. Note the position of Black's foot behind White's base leg.

5. Black completes the combination by continuing his forward motion until he is able to slam White down to the ground. Note that Black uses the bend of his front leg as found in the forward stance as a groin crushing technique on the downed White.

Step 1 *Rear Backfist/Downward Block to Spearhand Strike*

Step 2 & 3
*Rear Backfist/Downward Block
to Spearhand Strike*

Step 4 & 5 *Rear Backfist/
Downward Block to Spearhand Strike*

Spearhand Strike to Supported Outer Forearm Block

TECHNIQUE

Combination 4 – Spearhand Strike to Supported Outer Forearm Block

APPLICATION

1. White attacks Black with a same-side wrist grab. While this attack seems as though it would not have much of an effect on Black, White can use it to immobilize Black briefly so that he can attempt to strike him.

2. Black counters the wrist grab by using the blocking hand of the outer forearm block. Black places his blocking hand on top of White's attacking wrist and applies downward pressure while initiating the movement of the outer forearm block.

3. Black continues to keep contact on White's attacking wrist with his blocking arm while sliding the supporting arm underneath White's attacking arm.

4. Using the turning motion of the pattern, Black's supporting hand applies downward pressure to the back of White's shoulder, forcing him to bend forward. While the supporting hand is forcing White to bend forward, Black employs the blocking hand to the back of White's neck to further control his forward bend.

Step 1 & 2
*Spearhand Strike to Supported
Outer Forearm Block*

Step 3 & 4   *Spearhand Strike to Supported Outer Forearm Block*

Double Knifehand Block to Inverted Spearhand Strike to Rear Backfist/Downward Block

TECHNIQUE

Combination 5 – Double Knifehand Block to Inverted Spearhand Strike to Rear Backfist/Downward Block

APPLICATION

1. Black uses the double knifehand block to create space between him and White. In this way, White is unable to get the underhook with his right arm and will have greater difficulty securing a good grip on Black.

2. Black then uses the space created with the double knifehand block to drop and grab White's lead ankle in a wrestling technique called an "ankle pick." Black secures White's same-side arm so he cannot get a good grip on him and interfere with the technique.

3. Black then uses the rear backfist strike to pull the leg as he pulls down with his lead hand. These simultaneous motions pull White off balance and to the ground.

Step 1 *Double Knifehand Block to Inverted Spearhand Strike to Rear Backfist/Downward Block*

Step 2 & 3
*Double Knifehand Block to
Inverted Spearhand Strike to
Rear Backfist/Downward Block*

CHAPTER 13

Kwang-Gae

Kwang-Gae is the 10th pattern in the Taekwondo curriculum and
is the first black belt level pattern taught in many Taekwondo organizations. Kwang-Gae is named after the 19th king of the Koguryo Dynasty,
Kwang-Gae To Wang. Kwang-Gae is remembered for expanding the lands
of the Koguryo Dynasty to include two-thirds of what is known today as
Korea, Manchuria, and Inner Mongolia. The 39 movements in the Kwang-
Gae pattern represent both the number of years of Kwang-Gae's rule as
well as the first two figures of the year he became king, 391 A.D. The odd
shape of the pattern represents the king's broadening of territory. Kwang-
Gae introduces new movement techniques to the Taekwondo practitioner
such as forward double stepping, forward double stepping and turning, and
shifting stances. Offensively, Kwang-Gae introduces the concepts
of consecutive or double kicks (pressing side kick/side kick).

Knifehand into Palm to Reverse Upset Punch

TECHNIQUE

Combination 1 – Knifehand into Palm to Reverse Upset Punch

APPLICATION

1. White attacks Black with a twin wrist grab. This gives White the advantage of controlling Black's movement as well as taking away the use of his arms for counterattack and balance.

2. Black uses the upward swing of the circular knifehand strike to attack the weak part of White's grip, his thumbs. The result is Black freeing his hands from White's grasp.

3. As Black completes the circling portion of the knifehand strike and brings it into his palm, it results in White being slightly pulled off balance. Also note that White's left arm is bent in such a way that he does not have much power in attempting to escape while his right arm is trapped by Black's arms.

4. Black then executes the reverse upset punch while keeping his grip on White's wrist. The result is an elbow/shoulder lock on White's arm as well as a disruption of his balance.

Step 1 *Knifehand into Palm to Reverse Upset Punch*

Step 2 *Knifehand into Palm to Reverse Upset Punch*

Step 3 *Knifehand into Palm to Reverse Upset Punch*

Step 4 *Knifehand into Palm to Reverse Upset Punch*

Hooking Block to Low Double Knifehand Block

TECHNIQUE

Combination 2 – Hooking Block to Low Double Knifehand Block

APPLICATION

1. White attacks Black with a cross-side lapel grab. This attack gives White the ability to keep Black in a specific place while he attempts to strike him. White is also able to push Black backward, likely resulting in Black falling backward to the ground.

2. Black counters the grab by stepping to the outside of White's arm while executing the hooking block to White's arm near the elbow.

3. After moving to the outside and gaining control over White, Black initiates the low double knifehand block across White's throat while maintaining his grip on White's arm.

4. Black completes the low double knifehand block by pulling downward with his grip on White's arm while executing the block at a backward, downward angle. Note that Black uses his legs to sink into the technique so that his body weight is driving the technique rather than just his arms.

Step 1 *Hooking Block to Low Double Knifehand Block*

Step 2 *Hooking Block to Low Double Knifehand Block*

Step 3 *Hooking Block to Low Double Knifehand Block*

Step 4 *Hooking Block to Low Double Knifehand Block*

Pressing Palm to Pressing Palm

TECHNIQUE

Combination 3 – Pressing Palm to Pressing Palm

APPLICATION

1. Black uses a pressing palm technique to defend against White's same side lapel grab. Note how Black uses the knife edge of the pressing palm to attack White's biceps muscle. While this will not likely cause significant damage, it is quite painful and will cause White to move downward away from the pain. Also note that it is not the downward strike of the pressing palm that causes the reaction in White, rather it is the combination of the strike and the sinking of Black's weight into the strike as a result of him lowering his stance.

2. Black uses the second pressing palm against the side of White's head. Because White is already off balance from the first pressing palm, Black continues the motion in that direction. With White's balance disrupted, Black is now able to either escape or continue his counterattack by striking White's exposed ribs with a knee strike.

Step 1 *Pressing Palm to Pressing Palm*

Step 2 *Pressing Palm to Pressing Palm*

Supported Outer Forearm Block to Scissor Block

TECHNIQUE

Combination 4 – Supported Outer Forearm Block to Scissor Block

APPLICATION

1. Black attacks White with the supported outer forearm block in the form of a twin lapel grab with the blocking arm high on the lapel and the supporting hand low on the lapel near the belt. With this grip, Black is able to manipulate White's movements and is in a good position for many throws and takedowns.

2. Black then uses the scissor block to reverse his hand position on White's lapels. By pulling down with his high hand and looping it around the outside of White's head (note the elbow), Black has snared White with a loop choke. The low hand rises and catches White's other arm to prevent him from mounting any significant counterattack.

Step 1 *Supported Outer Forearm Block to Scissor Block*

Step 2 *Supported Outer Forearm Block to Scissor Block*

Twin High Punch to Twin Upset Punch to Front Kick

TECHNIQUE

Combination 5 – Twin High Punch to Twin Upset Punch to Front Kick

APPLICATION

1. Black uses the twin high punch as a twin lapel grab combined with a pushing attack. The purpose of this attack from a grappling perspective is to push White off balance so that he can follow up with subsequent attacks.

2. Black uses White's temporary loss of balance to secure double underhooks on White, thereby giving him control over White's movements.

3. Black uses the front kick to thrust his hips forward and past White's. It is the rechambering of the front kick that Black uses as the actual application. Black places his kicking leg behind White's foot and combines his foot placement with the leverage of his hips to force White backward and to the ground.

Step 1 *Twin High Punch to Twin Upset Punch to Front Kick*

Step 2 *Twin High Punch to Twin Upset Punch to Front Kick*

Step 3
*Twin High Punch to Twin
Upset Punch to Front Kick*

Po-Eun

The 11th pattern in the Taekwondo curriculum, Po-Eun, was the pen name of Mong Ju Chung, a 14th century scholar and poet of the Koryo Dynasty. He was well-known for his great intelligence, which he used to achieve the highest score possible on three civil service exams for the Korean government. His knowledge in many areas was widely known and trusted and he was often summoned by the King for various projects on the national scale. Also, in addition to being a top Confucian scholar, he was also a pioneer in the field of physics. Of all of his accolades, Po-Eun was most known and respected for his patriotism. It was in fact his strong sense of patriotism that led to his untimely death. A King from the Ri Dynasty tried to get Po-Eun to side with him concerning some matters of state. Po-Eun declined of course and the result was his being assassinated with an iron hammer on a bridge near the center of the city. The Po-Eun pattern follows a single horizontal line which represents the loyalty to his king that cost him his life. The Po-Eun pattern introduces many stationary hand techniques executed from a sitting stance such as wedging blocks, supported and angled punches, and ridgehand guarding blocks.

Double Upset Punch to Low Side Kick to Outward Knifehand Strike

TECHNIQUE

Combination 1 – Double Upset Punch to Low Side Kick to Outward Knifehand Strike

APPLICATION

1. Black uses the double upset punch to pull White off balance. The crane stance allows Black to use his knee as either a strike to the ribs to soften White before the technique or as a leverage point at White's hip around which Black will off-balance him.

2. With White pulled off balance in one direction, Black uses the low side kick as a way to drop his weight to pull White off balance in the other direction. Black keeps contact between the back of his leg and the back of White's leg while still pulling White off balance with the double upset punch.

3. Black then drives the side kick to the floor, pulling White's leg with it and taking him off balance while using the outward knifehand strike under White's arm to take White totally off balance. From the position in Step 3, Black can easily take White to the ground by using his momentum in the direction of the kick or he can sweep White's base leg out from under him and throw him backward.

Step 1
*Double Upset Punch to
Low Side Kick to Outward
Knifehand Strike*

Step 2 & 3 *Double Upset Punch to Low Side Kick to Outward Knifehand Strike*

Hooking Punch to Scissor Block

TECHNIQUE

Combination 2 – Hooking Block to Scissor Block

APPLICATION

1. White attacks Black with a same-side wrist grab that will allow him to pull Black off balance or prevent him from escaping a follow up striking attack.

2. Black defends the grabbing attack by circling his wrist clockwise around White's and performing the hooking punch. The punching motion allows Black to use his hips with his new hand position to grab White's wrist and pull him off balance.

3. Black completes the counterattack by using the scissor block to take advantage of White's off-balanced position. Black pulls down on the arm that he grabbed while using the scissor block to create upward pressure on the same arm. This motion allows Black to have control over the arm so that he can prevent White from escaping while countering with kicking attacks or with a turn of the hips into White's body, he can lock the shoulder.

Step 1 & 2
Hooking Block to Scissor Block

Step 3
Hooking Block to Scissor Block

Back Elbow to Sitting Stance Punch to Back Elbow to Side Punch

TECHNIQUE

Combination 3 – Back Elbow to Sitting Stance Punch to Back Elbow to Side Punch

APPLICATION

1. White attacks Black with a same-side wrist grab that will allow him to pull Black off balance or prevent him from escaping a follow-up striking attack.

2. Black uses the sitting stance back elbow as a defense against White's grab by stepping back, dropping his weight, and pulling his arm into his hip. These motions, when done together, give Black the power to pull White off balance and into his counterattack.

3. Once White is pulled off balance, Black uses the sitting stance punch to free his wrist from White's grasp. The force of the punch acts against the weakest part of White's grasp, the area where the thumb meets the fingers.

4. Black then uses the back elbow strike on the opposite side to pull White back into his hips to pull him off balance once again. Note that Black's arm position on White results in an elbow lock on White's arm.

5. Black finishes the combination by using the side punch to throw White to the side and completely off balance. Note that the position of Black's hands during the side punch locks White's arm and gives Black control over it. Black can either strike White in any of his now vulnerable areas or he may simply use his hips to turn and throw White to the ground.

Step 1 & 2
Back Elbow to Sitting Stance Punch to Back Elbow to Side Punch

Step 3 & 4
Back Elbow to Sitting Stance Punch to Back Elbow to Side Punch

Step 5
Back Elbow to Sitting Stance Punch to Back Elbow to Side Punch

Back Elbow to Supported Punch

TECHNIQUE

Combination 4 – Back Elbow to Supported Punch

APPLICATION

1. White attacks Black with a cross-side wrist grab. The danger of this attack for Black is that White can use it to turn Black's shoulder thereby giving White access to the back.

2. Black defends the grab by using the preparation of the back elbow strike to trap White's attacking hand and apply pressure to his wrist.

3. With White's wrist locked by the preparation of the back elbow strike, Black increases the pressure on the wrist lock by bringing his hands to his hips in the execution phase of the back elbow strike.

4. Black completes the technique by using the supporting punch to rapidly twist White's wrist. Note that the wrist lock shown with the supporting punch as a finishing technique will result in great damage to the attacker's wrist.

Step 1 & 2 *Back Elbow to Supported Punch*

Step 3 & 4 *Back Elbow to Supported Punch*

C-Block to Twin Back Elbow

TECHNIQUE

Combination 5 – C-Block to Twin Back Elbow

APPLICATION

1. White attacks Black with a cross-side wrist grab. In addition to turning Black, White can also use this grabbing attack to pull Black's arm across his body and get behind him through the use of a technique called the arm drag.

2. Black swings his arm into position for the C-block while stepping back and around to get his hips into the technique. The result is White's ribs are now exposed and Black has gained a hold of White's belt, allowing him to control White's hips.

3. Black uses White's temporary loss of balance and grip on White's belt to pull White in front of him so that he has taken White's back. Black has also gained a hold over White's lapels, with one hand slightly above the other.

4. Black then uses the motion of the twin back elbow strike to pull White's lapels across his throat in a scissor fashion resulting in a choking technique.

Step 1 & 2 *C-Block to Twin Back Elbow*

Step 3 & 4 *C-Block to Twin Back Elbow*

CHAPTER 15

Ge-Baek

Ge-Baek is the 12th pattern in the Taekwondo curriculum and typically the last pattern required for the rank of 1st degree black belt. Ge-Baek was a 7th century General of the Baekche Army most well-known for his defense against the combined attacks of the Silla and Dang Dynasties in 660. He was able to organize an army of 500 soldiers for a battle that he knew he was entering outnumbered and with very little chance of success. Even knowing this, he did not hesitate to charge into battle to defend his country. Before the battle, he stated "I would rather die than be a slave of the enemy" and proceeded to kill his wife and family to prevent them falling into enemy hands. While winning four smaller battles, eventually, Ge-Baek was pushed back and outnumbered 10 to 1; his soldiers fought valiantly but were soundly defeated; during the course of the battle Ge-Baek was killed while in combat with the enemy and died defending Baekche.

The Ge-Baek pattern is performed in a straight line as recognition of his unwavering loyalty and strict military discipline. The 44 movements of the Ge-Baek pattern introduce many new techniques to the Taekwondo practitioner. These include the twist kick, the double arc-hand high block, the 9-shaped block, and the extensive use of sitting stance combinations and blocking techniques.

High Block to Downward Block to Arc-Hand High Block

TECHNIQUE

Combination 1 – High Block to Downward Block to Arc-Hand High Block

APPLICATION

1. White attacks Black with a same-side wrist grab. With this attack, White can pull Black's arm across his body for an arm drag so that White can get to Black's back. White is also capable of stopping Black from escaping if he decides to strike Black.

2. Black breaks White's grip on his wrist by executing a high block against the attack, weakening White's grip and giving Black the opportunity to counterattack.

3. Once White grip is weakened with the high block, Black uses the downward block to free himself completely from the attack by attacking the weak point of the grip, the union of the thumb and fingers.

4. With White pulled forward and off balance, Black executes the arc-hand high block as a locking technique to White's shoulder while pushing his head away to further control his movement. From this position, Black can execute a more aggressive locking technique or he can simply strike and escape.

Step 1 & 2
High Block to Downward Block to Arc-Hand High Block

Step 3 & 4 *High Block to Downward Block to Arc-Hand High Block*

Upward Palm to Sitting Stance Punch to Downward Backfist

TECHNIQUE

Combination 2 – Upward Palm to Sitting Stance Punch to Downward Backfist

APPLICATION

1. White attacks Black with a same-side lapel grab. With this attack, White can attempt to push Black backward so that he will lose his balance and fall to the ground. However, the best use of this attack is for White to stop Black from escaping when he decides to strike Black.

2. Black counters the attack by using his upward palm strike as a lapel grab that is inside White's attacking elbow. In doing so, Black has slightly locked White's wrist and also has negated much of White's advantage by being in a good position to counterattack.

3. Black then uses the sitting stance punch as another grab to White's opposite lapel. Note how White's arm is twisted as a result of Black's hip action.

4. With White's arm now forced out of position and isolated away from his body, Black turns into White's arm and attacks it using the downward backfist and the supporting hand as a shoulder lock to pull White off balance and down to the ground.

Step 1 & 2 *Upward Palm to Sitting Stance Punch to Downward Backfist*

Step 3 & 4
*Upward Palm to Sitting Stance
Punch to Downward Backfist*

Twin High Punch to Arc-Hand High Block to Upset Punch

TECHNIQUE

Combination 3 – Twin High Punch to Arc-Hand High Block to Upset Punch

APPLICATION

1. Black uses the twin high punch as an off-balancing technique. By pushing forward, Black forces White backward making it difficult for him to mount a counterattack.

2. Once taking White off balance to the rear, Black uses the arc-hand high block to turn White's body and force him into a position where his weight is balanced on one leg.

3. With White's body twisted off balance, Black finishes the combination by using the upset punch to quickly spin White in the opposite direction to allow for the takedown.

Step 1
*Twin High Punch to
Arc-Hand High Block to
Upset Punch*

Step 2 & 3

Twin High Punch to Arc-Hand High Block to Upset Punch

9 Block to Low Double Ridgehand Block (Variation A)

TECHNIQUE

Combination 4 – 9 Block to Low Double Ridgehand Block (Variation A)

APPLICATION

1. Black attacks White with a same-side wrist grab. In doing so, he is able to affect the angle with which he faces White; thereby allowing him to attack White while avoiding White's weapons for counterattack.

2. Black then uses the circular nature of the 9 block to lock White's shoulder. This is accomplished by swinging the arm over White's arm and then around until the palm rests on the chest. Moving to complete the 9 block will pull White off balance even further.

3. Once the 9 block has been used to off-balance White, Black now begins to execute the low double ridgehand block.

4. Upon executing the low double ridgehand block, Black is able to completely disrupt White's balance backward and take White to the ground by pulling with both arms diagonally downward.

Step 1 & 2 *9 Block to Low Double Ridgehand Block (Variation A)*

Step 3 & 4
9 Block to Low Double Ridgehand Block (Variation A)

9 Block to Low Double Ridgehand Block (Variation B)

TECHNIQUE

Combination 4 – 9 Block to Low Double Ridgehand Block (Variation B)

APPLICATION

1. In another application of the 9 block to low double ridgehand block combination; Black attacks White with double lapel grab with one hand slightly higher than the other. This common grappling attack allows Black to enter into a number of throws and choking techniques.

2. Black uses the lapel grab to jerk White's head quickly downward. Black uses the high hand on the double lapel grab to loop a section of the gi under White's neck as he pulls him downward. In the alternate view, you can see that Black's grip on the lapel combined with the downward jerking motion and looping of the gi create a noose around White's neck.

3. With White securely trapped in the choke, Black may easily take a step back and transition to the low double ridgehand block and take White to the ground. From this position, Black can finish the choke or release it and escape.

Step 1 *9 Block to Low Double Ridgehand Block (Variation B)*

Step 2 *9 Block to Low Double Ridgehand Block (Variation B) (with alternate view)*

Step 3
9 Block to Low Double Ridgehand Block (Variation B)

ABOUT THE AUTHORS

TONY KEMERLY, PH.D. is an Associate Professor of Exercise Science and the Chair of the Department of Exercise and Sports Science at High Point University. He received his doctorate in biomechanics from The University of Mississippi. His martial arts experience includes the rank of black sash in Blue Dragon Kung Fu, and black belt ranks in Taekwondo with the World Taekwondo Federation, the International Taekwondo Federation, and Living Defense Martial Arts. Over the past five and a half years he has trained under the tutelage of Steve Snyder and Danny Dring in Brazilian jiu jitsu, earning the rank of purple belt. Dr. Kemerly lives in High Point, NC with his wife Trish and their two dogs, Mika and Ripley.

STEVE SNYDER co-owns and operates a full-time martial art studio with his wife, Mariea Snyder in High Point, NC. Together they have two children: Deven and Elizabeth whom are active martial arts; in addition to other sports. Steve's martial arts experience includes: black belts in TaeKwonDo, Weeping Style Jujutsu, Joe Lewis Fighting Systems, Bill "Superfoot" Wallace Systems, Branch's American Martial Art Systems, and brown belt in Brazilian jiu jitsu. He is one of the few martial artists to ever receive black belts under both Mr. Joe Lewis and Mr. Bill "Superfoot" Wallace. In 2008, Steve was named "Pound for Pound Fight Trainer of the Year" by Mr. Joe Lewis. Steve's martial art training is under the direction of Mr. Danny Dring from Sherwood, Arkansas. Mr. Dring's influence has contributed greatly to the enthusiasm and knowledge Steve carries in his martial art career.